Taking Narrative Risk

The Empowerment of Abuse Survivors

Lori L. Montalbano-Phelps

UNIVERSITY PRESS OF AMERICA,® INC.

Dallas • Lanham • Boulder • New York • Oxford

Copyright © 2004 by
University Press of America,® Inc.
4501 Forbes Boulevard
Suite 200
Lanham, Maryland 20706
UPA Acquisitions Department (301) 459-3366

PO Box 317
Oxford
OX2 9RU, UK

Library of Congress Control Number: 2004106591
ISBN 0-7618-2914-8 (paperback : alk. ppr.)

To the memory of my mother,
Anna M. Montalbano,
who never stopped believing in this project.

Contents

Preface

This book represents a revisiting of research that I began a decade ago. Specifically, the study examines personal narratives of abuse survivors and attempts to assess the relationship between narration and teller empowerment. Two groups of participants were included in the research. First, are clients of a local shelter for victims of domestic violence and abuse in Hammond, Indiana. Second, are self-selected volunteers, who requested to be a part of the study. The narratives include survival stories of rape, incest, and battery. The narratives were collected in personal interviews, transcribed and coded for emergent themes. This book examines the process of data collection and analysis and can be beneficial in coursework in communication studies, performance methodology and narrative analysis. Research for this study reinforces the notion that narrating their experiences assists the survivors in narrative sensemaking as well as in reinforcing their empowered stances. Narrative sensemaking is aided by the use of *survivor discourse*, thematic combinations, and dramatic references. Performative strategies include efforts to create characterization, a convincing story line, and setting the stage for their own transcendence. Through re-performance or staging of the narratives in a theatrical production, performers and directors for the show were able to analyze the process of empowerment. The rehearsal process accentuated the categories of disempowering and empowering themes that were found in the rhetoric of the survivors. Results of the study indicate that narrating experiences of victimization and abuse is a necessary step in moving from victimization to survivorship, and is consequently, an essential way for victims of abuse to become empowered. The narrators for this study became empowered through the performance and re-performance of their own survivor narratives, as they created and audienced their own storytelling performances. In the chapters that follow, the fundamental steps in acquiring narrative research is discussed including precautions and implications of conducting research on sensitive material. Additionally, the process of analysis is defined and applied to the narratives, highlighted by specific references and excerpts of the narratives collected. Names and any identifying details have been removed from the excerpts to protect the confidentiality of the participants. Finally, analysis is conducted in multi-dimensional ways including a rhetorical analysis of the content of the narratives, as well as a performative analysis of the narrators use of storytelling devices.

ACKNOWLEDGEMENTS

First and foremost, I must express gratitude to the courageous individuals who participated in this study. Without the contributions of their life stories, this book would not be possible. Next, I would like to acknowledge those who made the research and this study possible. In particular, Dr. Nathan Stucky, who directed the study, and additional members of my dissertation committee, Dr. Ronald Pelias, Dr. Mary Hinchcliff-Pelias, Dr. James Van Oosting, Dr. Kathryn Ward. To Chris Broda-Bahm, for her many contributions to this process, the production, and for her friendship. To Dr. Theresa Carilli, for her belief in this process. To Dr. Carol Benton for her assistance in scripting the material. To the Indiana University Northwest College of Arts and Sciences Faculty Development Committee for the grant. I would like to thank Cheryl Montalbano and Linda Cohen for their love and support. To Andrea Phelps-Fagin, who worked on manuscript preparation. To my husband, Mark, for his encouragement. To my children, Mark and Annie, for letting mommy finish what needed to be done.

Selected material in Chapters 2 and 3 is used by permission from Lawrence Erlbaum Associates.

Chapter One

Introduction to the Study

People tell stories to survive. Narrating experiences of victimization can help abuse survivors bring change to their lives. Robinson (1982) explains that "personal narratives are situated communications. They occur in distinguishable contexts of interaction and can be used for a wide range of pragmatic functions" (p. 58). Personal narratives contribute to the preservation of familial and cultural history, teaching and learning; they can entertain or amuse. Some personal narratives represent stories of survival that not only encourage the listener, but also empower the storyteller. As Richardson (1990) explains:

> Narration displays the goals and intentions of human actors; it makes individuals, cultures, societies and historical epochs comprehensible as wholes; it humanizes time; and it allows us to contemplate the effects of our actions, and to alter the direction of our lives (p. 117)

Personal narratives represent an important way of altering the direction of the life of an abuse victim. Often, victims of abuse are trapped in silence. Without the ability to narrate their experiences to family, friends, police officers, medical personnel or social workers, the abuse victim may remain victimized by the cycle of violence indefinitely. One abuse survivor explains why she told her story to her abuser's family: "I don't know how I expected them to save me, they didn't know how to save themselves, it happened to them. So, I thought maybe telling people would do it." This statement demonstrates the teller's conscious attempt to cope with an abusive situation through telling others. Prior research on personal narratives suggests that narrating one's experience can contribute to the narrator's ability to cope with difficult situations and may ultimately serve as an important protection from continued involvement in dangerous or unhealthy relationships (NiCarthy, 1987). This study examines how abuse victims use the narrative act to bring about change in their lives.

The telling of a personal narrative, such as an abuse narrative, can empower tellers by allowing the narrators to move their experiences into public attention, and receive assistance from a support network. In addition, narratives allow for the creation of a "future story" (Polkinghorne, 1988) in which victims of abuse can envision themselves as survivors, free from the hold of their abusers, and possibly plan the future action necessary to emerge as survivors. Finally, telling abuse survivor narratives can allow the teller to reconceptualize past experiences, which may be necessary to facilitate change in their lives, for example, a victim may stop blaming her or himself for the abuse. One survivor stated:

> I know a lot more than I did then. And it took a lot of groups, a lot of talking, a lot of—you've got to ask for help I learned that . . . I had to learn, hey, you're not a bad person—you're a good person.

Through telling her story, this narrator came to see her abusive experiences much differently. Domestic violence and abuse pervade our society According to Dodd (1991):

> An estimated 3 to 4 million American women are battered each year by their husbands or male partners . . . an estimated 3.3 million children witness domestic violence each and every year, and among families where such violence takes place, the children are at a far higher risk of suffering physical abuse and neglect—1500 percent higher (p. 1–2)

Further, Browne (1991) explains that over a twelve-year period, 38, 648 people were killed by their partners. Of these deaths, approximately 62 percent were women killed by men, and 39 percent were men killed by women. These staggering statistics demonstrate a significant need for greater understanding of domestic violence and abuse. While most of these people are not subjected to severe beatings on a regular basis, it would be difficult to find someone who has not been affected by violence, to some degree. Whether through personal experience or observation, domestic violence touches all of our lives.

Personal narratives of abuse survivors represent an important source of information concerning the plight of the abused. Hence, abuse survivors represent an important "community" of storytellers. Their survival may depend on their ability to narrate their experience.

For this study, I examine personal narratives of abuse survivors in an attempt to understand the relationship between narration and teller empowerment. The narratives I will analyze are personal experience stories gathered from interviews I had with survivors of domestic violence and abuse. The two populations of survivors with whom I conducted interviews were clients of Haven House, a shelter for victims of domestic violence and abuse, and self-selected volunteers, who requested to be a part of this study. In the following section, I explore the current research on personal narratives which helps provide a framework within which abuse survivor narratives may be understood. Additionally, I offer a preliminary discussion of excerpts of the interviews.

Personal narratives can add to our understanding of everyday life experiences. Barthes (1977) maintains, "the narratives of the world are numberless" (p. 77). Further, "telling stories about personal experience is a prominent part of everyday discourse, and competence in such narration is an essential skill for members of a speech community" (Robinson, 1981, p. 58). The telling of personal experience narratives can affect the lives of abuse victims to a significant degree. For example, for abuse victims, skill in narrative ability could mean the difference between remaining in or exiting an abusive relationship. Moving the site of an abuse victim's narration from the private sphere to the public sector could result in the establishment of a social network. Furthermore, successful narration could garner help from this network of social workers, police, and medical personnel, which may be necessary for the victim's ultimate survival. Langellier (1986b) explains that, "personal narratives appear at the juncture between public, cultural performances and everyday discourse, such as conversation and small group discussion" (p. 140). Through the telling of their personal narratives to diverse audiences, abuse victims can facilitate change in their lives. For example, the telling of narratives can bring change in the teller's self-perception. Turner (1981) contends that narrative invokes reflexive activity "which seeks to 'know' antecedent events and the meaning of those events" (p. 163). Further, he suggests, "narrative is knowledge emerging from action, that is, experiential knowledge" (p. 163). Hence, through self-reflexive activity, abuse survivors can change the way in which they view their experiences, a change that may be necessary to facilitate removal from the abusive relationship.

Research on personal narratives indicates that many variables affect the telling of personal experience stories and that performance of intimate narratives can result in a variety of benefits to the teller. In the following pages, examples drawn from research on battered women's experiences are used to explain how abuse survivors use narrative as a coping strategy and survival skill.

Sharing Personal Narratives

Any analysis of the sharing of personal narratives needs to account for a variety of variables that can influence the telling. Robinson (1981) explains:

> Personal narratives are situated communications; they occur in distinguishable contexts of interaction and can be used for a wide range of pragmatic functions. The situated character of speech exerts important constraints and form on personal narratives. A proper accounting of everyday storytelling, must take into consideration what story is being told, to whom, when, and for what purposes. Furthermore, the contributions of the audience must be given equal consideration to those of the speaker or narrator (p. 58–59)

Three primary factors contributing to the telling of personal narratives include the teller's willingness and ability to narrate his or her experience, the context of the telling, and the teller-listener interaction.

Teller's Willingness and Ability to Narrate

Perhaps one of the most significant factors contributing to the telling of personal narratives of abuse survivors is the willingness and ability of the narrators to describe their experiences. The telling of an abuse narrative can involve personal risk to the teller, which may include not only psychological stress, but the threat of physical injury as well. Because of the potential consequences of narrating their experience, some abuse victims never feel safe enough to narrate their story, and consequently remain in abusive relationships for the duration of their lives. For example, if an abuser has convinced the victim that sharing stories of abuse could result in increased severity or incidents of violence, the victim may continually remain silent. One interviewee describes why she felt unable to seek legal assistance and leave her abusive husband:

> The fear was more binding, he started threatening me about abducting the children, taking them to—he said, "children are lost in the United States every day, and they can't find them." He indicated that he had the world in his hand to take the children. He said he would take them somewhere that I could never find them. I felt that that lifestyle was worth putting up with—to keep my children. And, if it meant that I needed to be beaten to keep my kids, that I could accept that. Anything, so I wouldn't lose my kids.

The fear described in this quote demonstrates how a victim can feel trapped in silence. Abuse survivors may use narration for a variety of reasons. For example, a victim may seek emotional love and support from friends or family, to gain access to a shelter, to obtain medical attention, or police protection.

Yet, the accessibility of such support is contingent upon abuse victims' ability to narrate their experiences. Narrating such experience can involve greater risk, and thus, is significantly influenced by the victim's willingness to take such a risk and tell their story.

The life history of abuse victims or survivors influences their ability to narrate life experiences. Bauman (1983) contends that, "the life history of an individual and the structure and evolution of an individual's repertoire represent important contextual frameworks for understanding the place of folklore in human life" (p. 365) Similarly, those involved in abusive relationships, such as wife battering, find that any attempt at retaliation can be personally damaging within specific contexts:

> Spouses . . . have a personal history to their relationship. Their actions have had time to come under the control of the other's reactions. The wife's repeated complaint reaction to her husband's aggression strengthens or reinforces his aggressiveness in future episodes. In turn, her compliance is strengthened or reinforced by its immediate effect—the avoidance or termination of his hostility (Wiggins, 1983, p. 111).

Consequently, an abuse victim may fear the consequences of personal narration, and seek compliance (for example, through silence) to avoid violence. In addition, the admission of violence may be contrary to the individual's perception of "appropriate" behavior for a spouse or child, which could also result in silence. One interviewee explains:

> It was like when you get the house together, when you buy an investment like that together, it was like—you're doomed. And the meantime it didn't stop, the abuse didn't stop. It was strong mental and physical, I was still afraid of whenever he got mad or angry about something, my son was getting as tall as he was, or taller, he's like six-two, and in the meantime, I had like four girls in a row. And in a sense, I often wondered if it was just a blessing there was only one of the kind like him, so-to-speak, cause if I had to have four boys, oh God, will they be like this to their girlfriends or wives, you think about stuff like that.

This quote seems to reinforce the notion that "gender-specific behavior" is predictable. For example, if a dominant male in the household demonstrates certain behavior, the same sex child will act in similar ways. Hutchings (1988) explains that society, which is guided by the dominant culture "conveys messages, images, as to what a woman should be and what a man should be. This image reduces a woman to a secondary position and causes her to devalue herself" (p. 21). Such behavioral or role-oriented constraints may restrict the victim's willingness to seek help through narration. Within a patriarchal society, which promotes ideas such as gender-specific behaviors, i.e.

dominance and submission, a female victim may not seek help because she has labeled herself as the "fault" of her abusive experiences, or she may feel that she has no recourse due to her lack of status within society. A male victim may not seek help because of the stigma of male dominance and power, which is perpetuated by patriarchy. He may remain silent for fear of rejection, chastisement, or fear of failure. Alexander, Moore and Alexander (1991) found that in heterosexual couples where the male held conservative-traditional views and the female more liberal views, the "enculturation of patriarchal values does seem to have an impact on the increased likelihood of violence" (p. 666). Consequently, if an abuse victim deviates from the values perpetuated by patriarchy, she may be subjected to increased abuse. Alexander et al (1991) also maintain that, "researchers have indeed discovered that abusive men frequently espouse more traditional views about women than do non-abusive men" (p. 658). If these traditional views are shared by the victims, they may limit the victim's perceptions of alternative possibilities and may cause them to believe that the abuse is their own fault, for example:

> A woman who is struck or beaten, even once, finds herself in a paradoxical situation, she is shocked and incredulous that the man she loves, the father of her children, would treat her so. But having internalized the cultural norm that women are largely responsible for the success or failure of human relationships, she interprets her mate's behaviour as somehow her own doing (Hoff, 1990, p. 43)

This internalization of fault may result in silence on the part of a victim. This silence may further perpetuate the abusive incidents. The following excerpt of a printed narrative explains this problem:

> I also felt guilty. He said he wouldn't hit me because I wasn't a bad person, but then he did. What was this thing I had done? I could never find it, but there must be something really bad. You don't go around hitting people for no good reason. I didn't know that it was something within him (NiCarthy, 1987, p. 29)

Consequently, a victim who feels responsible for the abuse may not seek help. This silence can be damaging in other ways. Hoff (1990) explains that the lack of such narration can bring delusions of reconciliation to the abuser: "a battered woman's failure to communicate explicitly her feelings of anger and rejection about her broken marriage can result in her harbouring wishes for reconciliation based more on fantasy that reality" (p. 175). For example, one interviewee noted:

> People saw this man and would tell me, what you doing with this guy? He's nothing but a this and that, you know, I'm like, I don't know I don't know. It's

got to be a habit. I just don't know why I stayed with him. It's just something I can't—if he wasn't there, I missed him. But when he beat me up, I hated him. You know there was two sides to my husband, that alcoholic side and the drugs and there was him being sober. And, I guess that was what I was holding on to— that sober [   ]. And I kept thinking, well, he's gonna change, he's gonna change. If he sees the change in me, he'll change. Bullshit. Bullshit.

This quote demonstrates one victim's belief that her thoughts of reconciliation were based more on wishful thinking than the reality of the situation. She was holding on to a belief that her abuser would change.

Another significant factor that may impede the teller's willingness and ability to narrate is the private-public sphere distinction that is promoted by the dominant culture. This distinction promoted the belief that familial/ domestic problems are private matters and should not be discussed in the public sphere. For an abuse victim who embraces such ideology, the act of narrating one's personal experience outside of the private sphere may be inconceivable, and consequently, that individual remains silent. Langellier (1989) suggests, "personal narratives are also used at the intersection of private and public spheres where telling a personal experience is part of a social process of coping" (p. 264). Despite the potential coping strategies such narration could invoke, many abuse victims remain constrained and muted by the belief that the private and public spheres should remain separate. Another interviewee explains her reaction to the silence she could not break regarding experiences of incest with her grandfather:

Nothing was ever mentioned again, like it never happened. Ever. And, once I popped the cork, on this one event, all the rage came out and I would be driving with my father, I remember one particular instance, and I would say things like, I hope grandpa dies a slow, miserable, painful death—he's such a scum bucket, or whatever, and my father would reprimand me for speaking with disrespect. And, that was really, to me, that was just as hard. I used to do it on purpose, just to see the reaction, so, eventually it faded out and we just never talked about— I mean, it wasn't something I'd think about anyway, you know?

The private-public sphere distinction silenced this narrator for many years. This caused her further pain and made her emergence from victimization to survivorship more difficult to realize. Despite constraints imposed by the public versus private sphere distinction, many abuse victims eventually choose to tell their experiences. Whether the individuals narrate experiences to obtain assistance or offer advice to someone who shares similar experiences, the choice that they make can involve potential psychological and physical injury.

The Context of the Telling

The telling of a personal narrative is influenced by the cultural context in which the telling occurs. Rules, roles, and performance expectations help determine how the narrative is constructed and how it is received by members of a given society. Personal narratives represent examples of performance in everyday life. Peterson and Langellier (1986) suggest, "examining personal narratives as performance emphasizes its function as a signifying practice that does not merely represent a person or a lived world, but produces meanings which count as real or rational (p. 111). Similarly, Bauman (1986) notes, "oral performance, like all human activity, is situated, its form, meaning, and functions rooted in culturally defined scenes or events—bounded segments of the flow of behavior and experience that constitute meaningful contexts or action, interpretation, and evaluation," that "the structure of performance events is a product of the systematic interplay of numerous situational factors" (p. 3–4). These factors include the participant's roles and identities, the expressive means employed in performance, ground rules, norms and strategies for performance. Other factors include criteria for the interpretation and evaluation of a performance and the sequence of actions that make up the scenario (Bauman, 1986, p. 4). Rules governing human communication such as "appropriateness" of topic, occasion, setting, and the relationship of the interactants, can constrain the performance of narratives in everyday life. Langellier (1989) contends, "like all performance events, personal narrative is structured by the culture in which it operates. The performance approach attempts to index the ground rules constraining performance, for example, genre, shared social attributes and cultural values, and speech situation" (p. 255–256). These "ground rules" of performance of narrative can constrain abuse survivors, and limit their willingness to engage in such performance. However, when such performances are encouraged, these narrators are able to utilize the performative features involved in storytelling to emphasize their perspective, and maximize the persuasiveness of their claim. When such features are invoked, not only is the content of the message interpreted and evaluated, but also the performative acts which accompany the text. This is consistent with Bakhtin's notion of "heteroglossia," which suggests, "at any given time, in any given place, there will be a set of conditions that will insure that a word uttered in that place and at that time will have a meaning different than it would have under any other conditions" (Holoquist, 1981, p. 423). For example, the performance of an abuse survivor narrative is assigned meaning according to the performance context that accompanies the utterance. A performance of an abuse survivor's narrative and the assessment of the narrative performance could take into account the teller's relationship to the listener, the physical context surrounding the telling, for example location, time of day, room temperature, and so forth.

Additionally, Stucky (1993) explains, "taken in their native circumstances, interviews, stories, or personal narratives exist on the border between ordinary daily activity and marked performance" (p. 172). Consequently, the narrator's command of performance features such as, nonverbal communication, "believability," dramatic emphasis, and so forth, can contribute to another's perception of the narrator's experience, which could affect his or her request for assistance. For example, individuals possess differing degrees of effectiveness in storytelling. If, in fact, the narratives are being evaluated according to the "effectiveness" of the "performer," what happens to the individual abuse victim who does not possess effective storytelling capabilities, for example performer credibility, skill in language use, emphasis in tone and inflection, and so on? Are these narrators any less legitimate? What are the consequences of a "bad" performance? What are the potential consequences of breaking culturally established rules regarding the performance of narratives? How skilled must the listener be in discerning these rules?

Barthes (1977) reinforces the notion of narratives as rule governed: "it is impossible to combine (produce) a narrative without reference to an implicit system of units and rules" (p. 81). To become an "effective" storyteller in a given society, then, the narrator must understand what Bauman (1983) labels the "context of meaning," "the information one needs to know about the culture in order to understand the content, the meaning, the 'point' of an item of folklore, as the people themselves understand it" (p. 363). The notion that the interactants must understand and effectively adhere to the rules governing the performance of narratives is an important one to abuse survivors. If survivors break one or more of these rules, they may not be afforded "abuse survivor status," and thus may not be offered the assistance /support they need for continued survival.

In addition to rules, expected cultural roles regarding gender and status impact the telling of narratives as well. Peterson and Langellier (1986) suggest, "tellability in stories depends on the use of culturally salient materials. The result of this is the tendency to use sedimented meanings that already exist in a particular culture, telling a story is a way to 'fill in the situation' by generating a familiar context for action"(p. 108). The implications of this claim indicate that in order to claim membership in a particular group, for example abuse survivors, one must conform to socially constructed images or roles that have been put in place by the dominant culture.

The study of personal narratives relies, to a great extent, on an analysis of the contextual factors that accompany the utterance. Langellier (1986a) contends, "a performed text cannot be understood apart from its context" (p. 63). Similarly, Bauman (1989) argues that it is unproductive to study narrative "within a framework that excludes a serious attempt to comprehend all of the modern social conditions and the myriad ways that these forces impinge upon and transform the lifeworld of the people" (p. 174).

The abuse survivor narrative often raises questions of appropriate behavior of culturally defined rules and roles. For example, many people seem obsessed with the question, why would a battered woman stay? To answer this question, re-interpretation and re-evaluation of the victim's behavior is put into place, to make it "appear" consistent with the presupposed rules and roles. Loseke (1992) describes such a social construction:

> In the process of accounting for the unacceptable behavior of staying in a relationship containing wife abuse, claims-makers have constructed a new collective representation—a "battered woman." The fully described ideal type would be a woman of any age, race, social class, or marital status who was in the social roles of wife and mother. Such a woman would want to leave—or would want to leave if she was not so confused as the result of her victimization—but she would be trapped within her continuing and brutal victimization by economic and emotional dependence by friends and social service providers who refused to help and by her traditional beliefs. Such a woman would be isolated by others, and overwhelmingly fearful and emotionally confused. She would have little faith in herself and she would suffer from a range of physical and emotional illnesses that were understandable reactions to her plight (p. 28)

Here, Loseke (1992) describes the "ideal type" of a battered woman, according to socially constructed images of such an individual. While some abuse survivors may represent some of the criteria described by Loseke (1992), many abuse survivors may not necessarily match the socially constructed criteria. If abused individuals don't match these images, they may not be considered deserving of "battered-woman status," consequently, they may be considered undeserving of assistance. For example, such socially constructed images suggest that a battered woman should fulfill the "social roles of wife and mother." Hence, the woman "should" be a spouse or monogamous partner of the abuser, certainly not the "other lover" of a married man, or a person involved in a lesbian relationship. Further, she must be victimized by "economic and emotional dependence," that is, unable to make it on her own. Socially constructed images suggest that she must want to leave—if she wants to stay, "she must like it." And, of course, she must have low self-esteem. Such socially constructed images of domestic violence and abuse assume a heterosexual orientation, and offer no consideration for gay or lesbian individuals involved in abusive relationships.

The study of abuse survivor narratives requires researchers to recognize and acknowledge such socially constructed "images" in their analyses. In addition, a researcher might establish a clear understanding of the cultural rules and roles which governed the original telling of the narratives, before personal experience narratives can begin to be understood with any accuracy or sensitivity. Otherwise, presuppositions and stereotypes could result in a misconstrued notion of the abuse survivor's experience.

Teller-Listener Interaction

Narrative performance represents an interaction that occurs between a teller and listener. As Scholes (1981) suggests, "narrative is the sequencing of something for somebody" (p. 205). The interaction between the teller and the listener allows for the cooperative construction (or destruction) of the narrative, and can result in altered subsequent performances, which aim to increase positive evaluation of the teller by the listener. Destruction of a narrative can occur when unsympathetic listeners react negatively to the teller's story. Such negative reactions may silence future narrative opportunities for the teller. Duranti and Brenneis (1986) maintain that others "ratify" our communication, that the system or interaction "is something that is partly constituted, that is, made real, possible, and meaningful, through its use by particular actors at particular times and places" (p. 240). Similarly, Barthes (1977) suggests, "there is a donor of the narrative and a receiver of the narrative. In linguistic communication, je and tu (I and You), are absolutely presupposed by one another, similarly, there can be no narrative without a narrator and a listener" (p. 109). Whether the listener is another individual or the narrators themselves, the result of the interaction is a "collaboration" to produce a story (Sullivan, 1986, p. 117). Frank (2000) explains that:

> Storytelling is the recursive elaboration of the relationship between those sharing the story. Shared memories are made present . . . stories reaffirm what people mean to each other and who they are with respect to each other . . . when life is hard, stories can provide those in the storytelling relation with some distance from whatever threatens them (p. 354)

The listener becomes an active participant in the storytelling process, and consequently, can alter the outcome of the narrative performance. Mandelbaum (1989) suggests, "recipient's have resources with which they may actually initiate and work through with the teller, a change in the nature of storytelling, while the storytelling is in progress" (p. 114). Further, she contends that the "recipient's participation as 'co-author' of the storytelling is integral to working out what the event recounted is 'about'" (p. 124). This interaction can have serious consequences for abuse victims or survivors narrating their experiences. On the one hand, a sympathetic listener, for example, might encourage survivors to speak much more openly regarding their experiences, which could potentially facilitate gained support by the listener, and a more assertive stance by the survivors. On the other hand, non-sympathetic listeners may silence the narratives of abuse survivors altogether, or cause the abuse survivors to reconceptualize their experiences as lesser problems than they are, which could result in added psychological stress to the narrators.

Another interviewee explains the complications involved in narrating her experience to different audiences:

> When I knew what was going on, when it actually dawned on me that him hitting me wasn't supposed to happen, I tried to think about ways to get out of— ways to make it stop. Not ways to leave the marriage, but I thought—if I told people, that would do it. Who could I tell—so I told his family, or they witnessed it. And, I kept looking to be saved from this. I expected somebody to come along and go, "My God, do you see what's happening? Come on, you gotta go." I really thought that would happen. But his family got so used to his verbal aggressions, and his tantrums, and his this, and his that. I don't know how I expected them to save me, they didn't know how to save themselves, it happened to them. So, I thought that maybe telling people would do it, then I started wishing that he'd hit me harder, that he'd break a leg, that he'd hospitalize me, so that somebody would notice. So that it wouldn't just be [she's] making it up, [she's] crazy.

This excerpt is an example of how unsympathetic or unresponsive listeners can influence the telling of subsequent abuse stories. This narrator began hoping for physical evidence to support her story, to make it more "believable" to her audience.

Fine and Speer (1977) argue, "the structure of the performance event itself may be emergent, since the act sequence of the event and/or the ground rules of performance may shift as they are negotiated by performer and audience in a dynamic relationship" (p. 378). The "emerging" event can also influence the teller's willingness to engage a narrative. By supplying a supportive, non-judgmental environment for abuse survivors to narrate their experiences, the chances of a positive interaction, that can be somewhat empowering to the narrators, are much greater.

The reactions of various listeners may encourage the teller to alter her or his narrative. Lucaites and Condit (1983) describe a purpose of the narrative as the "specific function to enact interest or to wield power" (p. 99). In addition, Lucaites and Condit (1983) suggest "in rhetorical discourse, the narrator must select and integrate only those elements of a story that make it persuasive to a specific audience" (p. 95). This view is shared by Herrnstein-Smith (1981) who contends that that, "the form and function of any 'version' of a narrative will be a function of, among other things, the particular interests and functions it was designed to serve" (p. 217). Also, Kerby (1991) holds that narrative is "unavoidably selective" (p. 47). The implication of such contentions is realized in the actual performance of the abuse survivor narratives. The narrators may select the specific details to include or exclude in their narratives based on the listeners' identities, and the relationship the narrators share with these listeners. For example, the type of services the listener can provide for the teller influences the specific objectives/goals of the narrative. Abuse survivors may select different bits of information, and utilize different styles of delivery, when they tell their experience to a friend or relative from which they hope to gain love or support, or a social worker, medical practitioner, or police officer who can offer shelter, medical care, or protection from the abuser. Because of the different goals, and a desire to have the narrative accepted by the listener, the narrative may "become" more "effective" through multiple tellings. Stahl (1983) explains, "any single experience story tends to become increasingly polished in terms of form and style as the teller repeats it in varying contexts.The teller's retellings always consciously or subconsciously take into account the form, style, and context of the original telling" (p. 268–269).

The teller-listener interaction offers implications for the empathic response and evaluation of the narrative by the listener as well. Richardson (1990) suggests, "social and generational cohesion, as well as social change, depend on [this] ability to empathize with the life stories of others" (p. 127). This is of particular importance to abuse survivors whose safety may be contingent upon their listeners' sensitivity to and empathy for their experiences. Without an empathetic listener, abuse victims may encounter increased difficulty in achieving survivor status, that is, they may become empowered or disempowered through the dynamics of the interaction. Bauman (1986) contends, "from the point of view of the audience, the act of expression on the part of the performer is thus laid open to evaluation for the way it is done, for the relative skill and effectiveness of the performer's display" (p. 3).

Once again, the issue of the narrator's perceived effectiveness is raised. For abuse survivors, this perception can impact life or death decisions. If, for example, abused individuals narrate their experiences and are rejected by service workers (listeners) who could offer refuge to the narrators, the narrators may remain in abusive relationships believing they have no other recourse.

Personal Narratives and Change

Research on personal narratives suggests that the performance of personal narratives can result in a variety of benefits to their tellers. Benefits include giving meaning to the teller's experience and enhancing the teller's self-concept, which can potentially lead to teller empowerment.

Narrative Meaning

Narrative is the discourse structure in which human action receives its form
and through which it is made meaningful (Polkinghorne, 1988, p. 135). Bauman (1989) explains a concept of narrative that explores the structure of
signification:

> An alternative view, now beginning to attract more and more proponents, is that
> events are not the external raw materials out of which narratives are constructed,
> but rather the reverse: Events are abstractions from narrative. It is the structures
> of signification that give coherence to events in our understanding, that enable
> us to construct the interdependent process of narration and interpretation, a co-
> herent set of interrelationships that we call an "event" (p. 5)

This view acknowledges the need for an understanding of narrative, which
recognizes narrative as "a distinctive way of ordering experience and constructing reality" (Richardson, 1990, p. 118). Ong (1982) explains that narrators choose material to include, and "have a conscious or unconscious ration-
ale for the selection and shaping" (p. 13). It is through narrative construction
that the "reality" of the abuse survivor's experience is organized and made
meaningful. Richardson (1990) suggests, "telling one's story gives meaning
to the past from the point of view of the present and future" (p. 126). This
meaning is transferred and co-produced by the teller-listener interaction
through the use of symbolic material contained in the narrative discourse.
Scholes (1981) explains, "a story is a narrative with a certain very specific
syntactic shape which allows for or encourages the projection of human values upon this material" (p. 206). One interviewee explains how she was un-
aware of "warning signs" inherent in her abuser's behavior. However,
through reflecting on her past experiences, she is able to interpret them much
differently:

> Certain triggers started right around that time, you can't drive the car because,
> he would say, "its wear and tear on the vehicles." I was like, "this is a car, that's
> what cars are for." But he would get real upset, you know, if I would go any-
> where. And he would tell me these horror stories, like, what if you break down
> on the side of the road, and some man comes and kills you or rapes you, I mean,
> just these horror stories, and I was afraid then, to go out . . . I just, just kind of
> stayed to myself, I didn't go places, I was just kind of not allowed to drive,
> have friends over, talk on the telephone. I mean, these were almost like un-
> stated rules. He would show his, his indignation to those kinds of things, in be-
> ing kind of forceful walking around, and that kind of thing. But it was never in
> your face, and it was never stated. Its just, that if you do these things, you know
> you will displease me, okay, so I guess that's when that whole manipulation

thing started—although it probably started way before then and I just didn't identify it.

In this passage, the narrator explains how she now reconceptualizes certain behaviors of her abuser. She is able to rethink the experiences and reify his behavior through narration of her experience. Through self-reflexive activity, narrators can assign new "meaning" to past experiences.

Sullivan (1986) suggests, "stories work unobtrusively to endow human life with meaning; they function through conscious processes embedded in the form" (p. 128). Similarly, Langellier (1989) adds, "narrative performances participate in the ongoing ideological struggle for meaning" (p. 268). Through narrative performances, abuse survivors are able to understand their experiences, and relate them in meaningful ways to their listeners. Polking-horne (1988) explains that narration "provides a framework for understand-ing the past events of one's life and for planning future actions. It is the pri-mary scheme by means of which human existence is rendered meaningful" (p. 11). The implications of this claim for abuse survivors are significant, be-cause through the act of narrating their life experiences, abuse survivors may come to understanding these experiences differently. These new perspectives can open up possibilities for action that they may not have considered prior to the narrative event. Furthermore, they may allow the listeners greater un-derstanding of their own experiences through the telling of their narratives. Polkinghorne (1988) claims, "narrative is the fundamental scheme for linking individual human actions and events into interrelated aspects of an under-standable composite" (p. 13). Through the narrative event, abuse survivors may provide information to their listeners which breaks down stereotypes and answers questions, such as, why the victims stayed in abusive relationships as long as they did. Fisher (1989) explains how the "traits" of the human condi-tion can be manifested through narrative performance:

> Regardless of the form they may assume, recounting and accounting for are sto-ries we tell ourselves and each other to establish a meaningful life-world. The character of narrator(s), the conflicts, the resolutions, and the style will vary, but each mode of recounting and accounting for is but a way of relating a "truth" about the human condition (p. 6)

Similarly, Kerby (1991) suggests, "in the case of our personal narratives, 'truth,' becomes more a question of certain adequacy to an implicit meaning of the past than of a historically correct representation or verisimilitude" (p. 7). In the fol-lowing excerpt, one narrator explains this process:

> I think its sad to know the reaction of some of my friends when I first came back and told them what had happened. They didn't understand that people, in those

situations don't tell anyone. They don't understand why. Some education has to happen there because I'm talking to college graduates who don't know that—they don't understand how it can happen to a strong-willed person. They don't understand how it can happen to an educated person . . . I think there is still a lot of stereotypes there. I think there is still a lot of blame that happens, a lot of self-blame initially. There's so much to explore, and it's not new. Its not new, it's our awareness that's new.

This narrator describes a need to educate others about the "truths" of abusive situations. Consequently, abuse survivors may use narration as a means of creating meaning or perceived "truths" of their lives. In addition, they may attempt to break down negative predispositions or impressions (of the narrator) held by the listeners, in an attempt to gain shared understanding of their experiences.

The nature of language itself contributes to the construction of meaning in narration. Kerby (1991) contends, "language is viewed not simply as a tool for communicating or mirroring back what we otherwise discover in our reality, but is itself an important formative part of that reality" (p. 2).
Through the performed language of narrative discourse, which is selected by the narrator, the narrator not only creates meaning for the teller and the listener, but for their social world. Langellier (1986a) maintains, "performance accomplishes a social use, it holds society together, helps reconnect alienated individuals, and engenders fresh social views" (p. 64). Similarly, Bauman (1989) explains how narratives construct social reality:

> When one looks to the social practices by which social life is accomplished, one finds—with surprising frequency—people telling stories to each other, as a means of giving cognitive and emotional coherence to experience, constructing and negotiating social identity . . . investigating the experimental landscape within moral significance in a way that can be brought to bear on human behavior (p. 113)

Hence, the transformative possibilities of constructing meaning in an individual's life extend to the social world in which the individual exists. Narration is an act that can indeed engender "fresh social views" on domestic violence and abuse, which may involve a "breaking" of the silence of abuse and encourage more involvement by the public sector. Understanding the "collective story" (Richardson, 1990, p. 128) of a group of individuals requires an examination of the individual's construction of meaning. Narrative serves that function for individuals. "It is in and through various forms of narrative emplotment that our lives . . . our very selves—attain meaning" (Kerby, 1991, p. 4). The construction of meaning through narration can result in an enhanced self-concept, and perhaps, empowerment of the abuse survivor.

Narration and the Teller's Self Concept

The telling of personal experience narratives can shape the teller's identity, and can enhance the teller's self-concept. Polkinghorne (1988) claims "we achieve our personal identities and self-concepts through the use of narrative configuration, and make our existence into a whole by understanding it as an expression of a single, unfolding story" (p. 150). The notion of an unfolding story can be quite encouraging to victims of abuse, who may have believed that no opportunities for change existed for them. The concept of self, then, "is not a static thing nor a substance, but a configuring thing of personal events into a historical unity which includes not only what one has been, but also anticipations of what one will be" (Polkinghorne, 1988, p. 150). The anticipation of what we will be emphasizes the notion of self-in-process that can lead, not only to improved self-esteem, but possibly empowerment of the narrator as well.

Norton (1989) echoes this theme, suggesting that stories "hold life together" (p. 182). Further, she claims "they form the building blocks of life, helping us lay foundations for our identity. If the structure is strong, the individual will thrive, if it is weak, the individual falters" (p. 182). Similarly, Kerby (1991) suggests, "self understanding and self identity will be dependent . . . on the coherence and continuity of one's personal narrative" (p. 6).

Stories, then, seem to serve important functions in an individual's self-perception. This function is apparent in the following passage of an abuse survivor:

> I know a lot more than I did then. And it took a lot of groups, a lot of talking, a lot of—you gotta ask for help. I learned that I was always the type of person—I didn't want anybody to know what he was doing. I wanted them to think our relationship was going so good, you know. We didn't have want for nothing. But inside, I was dying, dying—wanted to kill myself, maybe think it would be better if I wasn't alive. . . . I had to learn, hey, you're not a bad person—you're a good person. I'm what they call a survivor, and I'm gonna survive. I don't need a man to tell me this—sure I want that, man figure there, but not that bad. I used to think I had to have it, cause everybody else had 'em. No, now, that's all through.

In this quote, the narrator has redefined herself as a survivor and projects a future self-image, which demonstrates high self-esteem and a belief that she can make it without her abuser (or any other man in her life).

Personal narratives emphasize the individual in personal experience Langellier (1989) contends:

> In narratives of personal experience, the narrative event emphasizes the personal as it features a first-person narrator . . . relating an experience from his or her perspective. The narrated event highlights the experience because the event it

retells is from the teller's own life. The effect of telling a personal narrative is to enhance experience as expressivity exceeds referentiality to create a possible world (p. 255)

By emphasizing the individual in their narratives, abuse survivors can create such a possible world. The possible world created through narrative is especially significant for persons who are constrained by traditional roles perpetuated by dominant culture. Denzin, (1984) explains that violence occurs in unequal relationships:

> Violence occurs within an interactional framework of superordinate and subordinate relationships . . . cultural, social, legal, economic, and etiquette practices place the male in the dominant position . . . transforming him into a guest who is served, his spouse into servant-mistress, and the house into a residential hotel. When the understandings that underlie this interactional order are broken, violence is produced (p. 486)

These restrictive roles may be so internalized by those involved in abusive relationships that they may not recognize the potential "emerging self" that may be available to them through the narration of their experience. Further constrained by closed-minded positivists claims, such as "natural" differences, which "exist" between men and women, some abuse victims may fail to see the narrative possibilities available to them, which could aid in a certain self-transformation for the victim.

Sedlak (1988) describes the counseling methods that are often used to provide service to a battered woman:

> Typical goals in counseling a battered woman include decreasing her psychological dependence on the abuser, helping her to realize that she is not a helpless victim, but does have power over her own life, reestablishing her self-esteem, combating traditional sex-role concepts and any concomitant tendency to blame herself or to rationalize her abuse, dissuading her of beliefs that she can control the abuse, and decreasing her acceptance or tolerance of the use of physical force in interpersonal disputes (p. 336).

The counseling goals described by Sedlak (1988) in this passage seem obtainable through encouraging abuse victims to narrate their experiences. Through narration, abuse victims can construct their self-images, and recognize the power they harness over their own lives. According to research on personal narratives, an individual can re-establish his or her self-esteem, which is a primary goal for improving the life experiences of abuse victims. Hoff (1990) explains, "battered women leaving a violent relationship are in a 'liminal; or transition phase" (p. 170). In addition, Hoff (1990) suggests:

If a woman cannot successfully resolve the different changes that violence forces on her; she may remain in a 'liminal' state indefinitely, neither completely separated from here past nor ready to be incorporated into the community with new status and sense of self (p. 173)

Without transcendence from this liminal state, the victim may never achieve the sense of self as survivor.

It is through ascension from this "liminal" phase that abuse victims may re-define the self-concepts, and, perhaps, become empowered (through narration and other means) to the status of abuse survivors.

Narrative Empowerment

Narrating one's life experience can contribute to a transition from abuse victim to abuse survivor. This important source of empowerment is manifested in the "future story" described in narrative accounts of experience. Polkinghorne (1988) suggests, "the future story . . . requires an open and adaptive character" (p. 107). In addition, Polkinghorne (1988) warns, "if a person fails to project a hopeful story about the future, he or she undergoes a second kind of unhappiness, a life without change" (p. 107). An unchanged or unadaptive character represented by a future story which "attempts to maintain an un-changed self leads to unhappiness with the future" (Polkinghorne, 1988, p. 107). Research on personal narratives suggests that the telling of a personal narrative, such as an abuse survivor narrative, can empower the teller by al-lowing the narrators to move their experiences into public attention and re-ceive the understanding of others (Frank, 1995; Langellier, 1989; Park-Fuller, 1995; Plummer, 1995).

Any narrator, and this is particularly important for those who experience abuse or are recently removed from an abusive relationship, can use the nar-rative act to plot out who he or she may become. Kerby (1991) explains, "the stories we tell are part and parcel of our becoming. They are a mode of vision, plotting what is good and what is bad for us, what is possible, and what is not—plotting who we may become" (p. 54). Narrators can partake in such a transformation through the use of metaphoric language and the process of performing their narrative discourse. Norton (1989) claims that individuals use metaphor in everyday life to articulate the perception they have of the world, that "people possess metaphorical structures that define the way they cope . . . metaphor subtly empowers people with the ability to change their identities, their lives, and their interactions with others. As people craft metaphors, they also craft their lives" (p. 192). One interviewee described her transformation from victim to survivor. She states, "I feel like . . . a caterpil-lar who has become the butterfly." The selection of details and the structure of language used by the teller can lead to empowerment through narrative performance.

Langellier (1986a) contends, "viewed as socio-political action, the performance of literature gives voice to marginal and muted groups" (p. 64). Telling survivor narratives can serve a similar function. Abuse victims represent a muted group in that they are often trapped in silence for fear of consequences. Because of this, the act of narrating can be quite empowering to them. Hoff (1990) explains, "to move from the pre-battering phase of the women's lives to their accounts of the violence they experienced, reveals the relationship between violence and depression. The dynamic interplay between depression and violence is most acute when violence is treated as a private matter rather than a public issue" (p. 32). The sense of entrapment in an abusive relationship, with little hope for recourse, can disempower an abuse victim. In a letter, one victim explains:

> As a married woman I have no recourse but to remain in the situation which is causing me to be painfully abused. I have suffered physical and emotional battering and spiritual rape all because the social structure of my world says I cannot do anything about a man who wants to beat me. Society says that I must be committed to a man without any opportunity for an education and earning capacity. That my children must be subjected to the emotional battering caused when they see their mother's beaten face or hear my screams in the middle of the night. I know I have to get out but when you have nowhere to go you know that you go on your own and with no support. I have to be ready for that. I have to be ready to completely support myself and my children and provide a decent environment. I pray I can do that before I am murdered in my own home (Anonymous, U.S. Commission on Civil Rights, 1978).

This narrator's account of her experience vividly presents the sense of entrapment she feels. She indicates that societal and economic factors have stifled any possibilities for recourse. Further, this excerpt indicates a high level of disempowerment of the speaker. The narrative may serve to empower victims by allowing knowledge of the abuse or violence they experience to move into public attention. Hence, abuse survivors won't be trapped in a "private" silence.

The personal narrative can serve a certain rhetorical function as well. Kirkwood (1992) explains the rhetorical function of expressing possibilities through narrative to a listener:

> The role of rhetoric in expressing and applying the shared values of communities has long been acknowledged. An equally important role lies in acquainting people with creative possibilities of awareness and action. By helping people examine possibilities which previously they did not imagine or think they could

achieve, rhetors can free them to pursue satisfying responses to both personal and public needs (p. 44)

The telling of personal narratives can serve "possibilizing" functions for the narrator as well. As the narrators explore possibilities through the narrative event, they become audience to their narratives, and can gain empowerment through articulation of their own ideas.

The telling of narratives can change the direction of the teller's life. Richardson (1990) maintains that narrative "allows us to contemplate the effects of our actions, and to alter the directions of our lives" (p. 117). This change can empower a victim of abuse, but it cannot be achieved without involving some personal risk. NiCarthy (1987) explains, "it's hard to admit out loud that you've been mistreated by someone you love or 'need,' but it's also the beginning of your best protection" (p. 296). NiCarthy (1987) also suggests "stories manifest an individual's way of coping. By telling a story, an individual takes positive steps to cope with what happened (p. 128). One interviewee explains:

> I started going to ACOA — Adult Children of Alcoholic's twelve step group, as a support system, so that I could talk to other people, even though their situation may not be exactly like mine, I knew that a lot of feelings that they had would be. So, that was terrific, I met some friends who would not judge me, who listened, reasoned things out, provided me with hope — through their experiences. And then, I showed up at those meetings. First, all I did was listen, and then all I did was cry, and then I cried and talked intermingling, and then I talked. And then I found out I provided other people with some hope — and that just amazed me, that I could do that. Because, I felt so powerless, so helpless, so defen — I had no way of defending myself, I expected everybody else to do it. I knew that part of my healing process was to remember why I married this man, and I forced myself to do that. To remember that he was charming, and I felt I really needed to verbalize it.

In this excerpt, the narrator describes the evolution of her ability to narrate her experience and emphasizes the positive outcome of her storytelling. This reinforces NiCarthy's (1987) contention that describing the abuse orally is an important step to coping with what happened.

Further, NiCarthy (1987) explains, "in deciding to leave abusive partners, some women seem to experience a sudden breakthrough, similar to the 'snapping out' phenomenon in which people 'suddenly' come out of a trance like state induced by some religious cults" (p. 310). This breakthrough, or emergence, is a transition that seems to move the abuse victim to the status of survivor. By reconceptualizing and articulating their experiences through narration, abuse survivors can come to see their experiences in entirely new ways that contrast earlier perceptions, for example, that they were somehow re-sponsible for the abuse they experienced.

Additionally, abuse survivors may need to alter the perceptions of their lis-teners. Narration can facilitate this objective as well. "Throughout the telling . . . narrators seek not only to explain an experience, but guard it from hostile criticism and protect their version of the truth, steering their audience to share their interpretation and their philosophy" (Bennet, 1986, p. 432). By explain-ing their experience to others, or convincing others of their "version" of their experience, abuse survivors can become further empowered.

Important questions regarding the telling of abuse survivor narratives need to be considered. In the following chapters, I will examine these questions: What role does narrative risk play in the narratives of the participants of this study? How does the telling of abuse survivor narratives impact the teller? What can we learn about highly disclosive narratives through re-performance of abuse narratives? In Chapter Two, I will clarify the methodological proce-dure used for gathering and analyzing the data for this study.

Chapter Two

Methodological Procedures

INTRODUCTION

Examining abuse survivor narratives requires both responsibility and sensitivity on the part of the researcher. Past research on methodological procedures and practices demonstrates a significant need for accountability to the participants. In a study of personal narration, such accountability includes consideration of the diversity of the population of participants, as well as sensitivity to the personal involvement and personal risk taken during times of intimate disclosure. Variables such as race, class, gender and biological sex of the narrators are important factors to acknowledge when formulating and carrying out methodological procedures. In this chapter, I will discuss the assumptions and precautions, which guided the formation of the methodology and subsequent analysis of the survivor narratives. Additionally, I will explore the contributions of performance as a method of inquiry in the analysis of narratives. Finally, I will describe the specific methodology involked for the analysis of the abuse survivor narratives collected for the study.

Methodological Assumptions and Precautions

Prior research on methodological procedure yielded the formation of assumptions and precautions that guided the research for this study.

Assumptions

Issues such as entitlement (Schuman, 1982), transformative possibilities, and the narrators' biological sex, are important to the analysis of the survivor narratives. While these topics are diverse, their impact on methodological

practices is significant. A discussion of a feminist critical approach to such issues is valuable to a researcher examining abuse survivor narratives.

Entitlement

Entitlement issues concern who has the right to speak and who is silenced
within a society. Langellier (1986) contends that exploring "personal narratives raises issues of public policy and ethics, for example, the unequal distribution of storytelling rights according to status and power, the dichotomy
of public and personal experience, and gender, class, and ethnic differences
in storytelling" (p. 141).

Abuse victims are not always afforded storytelling rights. If, as a class of
people, abuse survivors are silenced, the implications invoked upon the individual who deviates from such "norms" imposed by society, are significant.
That is, if individuals choose to narrate material publicly which is considered
to be "normally" private material, the narrator could risk rejection, chastisement, or other unsympathetic responses to their disclosure. Such risk should
not only be recognized and acknowledged by the researcher, but perhaps, play
a vital role in the analysis of the narrative performance as well. Conquergood
(1983) explains that, "much of the work in oral history and oral tradition is
motivated in part by a need to rescue from invisibility vast numbers of people" (p. 149). Consequently, the research procedure itself, for example, the interview process that yields abuse narratives, can in part, serve the important
function of giving voice to a "muted group."

Nelson (1989) states, "what is required is that the methodological principles that inform the doing of research not sever the phenomena from the
method. The phenomena should be permitted to speak for themselves and
thus guide the construction of methodological theory and procedure" (p. 238).
Hence, the research method should be designed to promote entitlement rights
for the narrators/subjects. Langellier and Hall (1989) explain how such a
methodology can work for a group of subjects, for example, research on
women's communication: "research for women does not simply generate new
knowledge about women for the sake of knowledge, but conducts research
with the purpose of empowering women" (p. 195). With such research objectives in place, the researcher and subject can collaborate to learn more about
the topic under investigation. Spitzack and Carter (1989) claim that despite
traditional research which is committed to "objectivity," and promoting separation between the "knower and the known," "feminist research reveals that
the researcher and the researched cannot be separated, they are both en-
meshed in the socio-cultural world. Feminists argue that subjects can speak
for themselves, and can lead insight to scholarly endeavors" (p. 35). Research

objectives, which acknowledge the teller-listener interaction that occurs between the researcher and the subject, as well as highlighting the interviewees' voices, can facilitate further empowerment of the subject. For example, facilitating an interpersonally sensitive environment can allow for the disclosure of highly personal information in a non-threatening, non-judgmental manner, which could promote a reconceptualization of the abusive experiences by the narrator. Hence, the narrator is placed in an empowered position in the interview situation. Such an environment can yield important information about the survival of violence and other abuse. Consequently, it is important for any researcher examining the personal narratives of abuse survivors to allow the insights of the individual narrators speak for themselves. The interconnected relationship that can exist between the researcher and the interviewee needs to be acknowledged, and a researcher should avoid futile attempts at pure objectivity, and instead, recognize the mutual construction of the narrative experience. Consequently, assuring entitlement rights of informants is a vital concern.

Transformative Possibilities

The research approach can facilitate the transformation of the subject through the narrative process. One site of transformation resides in the language. Capo and Hantzis (1991) explain that language can be a site for radical change, "claiming language a locus for revolution, feminist critics continue to enact resistance, by inventing linguistic forms that employ imaginative gestures while eluding the logical balance, descriptive simplicity, oppositional structures, and forced closure of earlier rhetoric" (p. 253). Consequently, not only can the narrative act be transformative, but the research experience can be as well. The transformative possibilities reside in both the language of the narrator as well as the language of the researcher. Hoff (1990) suggests, "if scientific reporting obscures the voices of those researched, some of the study's value is also lost . . . knowledge from research should benefit those researched" (p. 14).

Richardson (1990) explains that the membership of an individual narrative in a larger collective story can be transformative as well:

> at the individual level, people make sense of their lives through the stories that are available to them, and they attempt to fit their lives into the available stories . . . collective stories which deviate from standard cultural plots provide new narratives, sharing them legitimates a replotting of one's own life. New narratives offer the patterns for new lives. The story of a transformed life, then becomes part of the cultural heritage affecting future stories and future lives (p. 129)

Consequently, with more research on issues such as domestic violence and abuse, comes more opportunities for individuals to participate in the collective story, and become encouraged and empowered by others who have transformed their lives. By providing narrative opportunities, such research contributes to the body of narratives that emerge from the private sector into public knowledge.

Biological Sex of the Narrator

An important consideration for the analysis of personal narratives, including abuse survivor narratives, is the biological sex of the subject. Some research indicates that sex differences can impact narrative style and delivery, and researchers are cautioned not to generalize over sex or gender lines. Presnell (1989) explains that an oral/literate distinction exists regarding the narrative behaviors and styles of women and men. Presnell (1989) contends characteristics of women's storytelling exist when "themes are reiterated in multiple forms, situational factors play a significant role, and a high degree of involvement is apparent. These correspond to the episodic structure, high context coding, and high involvement of oral discourse style" (p. 128). Men, according to Presnell (1989), argue linearly to solve the "problem of a moral conflict, generally arriving at a definite conclusion, situated features are minimized . . . and distance ("objectivity") is established to distance oneself from personal involvement in the decision making process itself" (p. 128). Furthermore, Presnell (1989) warns, "if a literate model is adopted to study women's oral traditions, distinctive characteristics of women's communication could be systematically overlooked" (p. 131). This view is shared by Langellier and Hall (1989), for example, who suggest, "interviewing women for personal narratives [also] requires attention to the communicative norms of women's storytelling" (p. 204). Consequently, sex specific characteristics in storytelling processes could represent an important variable in the analysis of abuse survivor narratives.

Gender roles promoted by the dominant culture, also influence narrative performance, and represent another set of variables a researcher should consider in her or his analysis of narrative content and the narrative act. Such variables may include constraints on assertive or proactive behavior, "appropriateness" in behavior based on biological sex, limitations on behavior based on gender "ideals," and so forth.

The Convergence of Race, Class, and Gender

In studies involving human subjects, issues of race, class, and gender can have important influences on data collection and the interpretation of data.

Research on the convergence of these variables demonstrates a need for careful consideration of the demographic background of the participants and researchers for any given study. Much of past research, however, including some feminist theory, has been exclusionary in design. Exclusionary research of the past often focused on issues relevant to white middle-class individuals. The results were findings that had little or nothing to do with the experiences of diverse populations that make up American culture. Baca Zinn, Weber Cannon, Higginbotham, and Thornton Dill (1986) explain the dangers of perpetuating exclusionary research:

> Practices that exclude women of color and working class women from the mainstream of women's studies have important consequences for feminist theory. Ultimately, they prevent a full understanding of gender and society. The failure to explore fully the interpreting of race, class, and gender has cost the field the ability to provide a broad and truly complex analysis of women's lives and of social organization. It has rendered feminist theory incomplete and incorrect (p. 295)

Similarly, Hill Collins (1991) explains how research generalizations can suppress diverse groups such as African American women:

> Women's studies has offered one major challenge to the allegedly hegemonic ideas of elite white men. Ironically, feminist theory has also suppressed Black women's ideas. Even though Black women intellectuals have long expressed a unique feminist consciousness about the intersection of race and class in structuring gender, historically, we have not been full participants in white feminist organizations. . . . Themes advanced as being universally applicable to women as a group on closer examination appear greatly limited by the white, middle class origins of their proponents (p. 7)

In an effort to be more inclusive, researchers must include a diverse population of participants in their research. Walker (1983) explains:

> What is always needed in the appreciation of art, or life, is the larger perspective. connections made, or at least attempted, where none existed before, the straining to encompass one's glance at the varied world the common thread, the unifying theme through immense diversity (p. 5)

Similarly, Ward (1993) explains the importance of inclusionary practices, utilized to yield various perspectives on life experiences:

> I argue that emerging inclusive feminist theories that have questions of race, class and gender at their core, will provide more accurate ways of looking at our world. As such these theories do not seek to provide a "complete" picture of the

world, but outline various standpoints/perspectives as provided by combinations
of race, class, and gender (p. 365)

Recognizing the convergence of race, class, and gender is important to the
analysis of personal narratives. Apetheker (1989) explains that women's
storytelling reflects their social reality. This social reality, according to
Apetheker (1989), is "reinforced by class, by race, by the prescription of
gendered roles, inscribed in the dailiness of women's lives" (p. 40).

Exclusionary research practices fail to acknowledge how the intersection
of demographic variables influence data collection and analysis. Domestic violence and abuse know no boundaries. They are influenced by gender roles
and occur across diverse racial and socio-economic classes. Including the experiences of a diverse population is necessary to provide more accurate findings in research on domestic violence and abuse. Such inclusionary practices
can yield greater insight into the ways specific narrators use the narrative
event to facilitate change in their lives.

Research Precautions

Abuse survivor narratives represent stories filled with rich yet very sensitive
and potentially risky information. Hence, a researcher should acknowledge
the potential risks and consequences involved for the tellers as they communicate their life stories to others. The researcher must handle the narrative
with care and sensitivity (Denzin and Lincoln, 2000). Conducting research on
abuse survivor narratives requires accountability to "the other" as well as sensitivity on the part of the researcher. Langellier (1989) contends:

> Researchers, as well as narrators and listeners are implicated in existing systems
> of power and knowledge. To be ethically responsible in studying personal nar-
> ratives, researchers must take care not to reproduce in scholarship the social dif-
> ferences . . . that mark Otherness and participate in oppressive systems (p. 271).

Hence, researchers must examine their own motives and objectives to ensure
accountability to the other.

The use of abuse survivor narratives in the study of personal narratives itself is debated by some researchers. Robinson (1981) describes the implications of such research:

> Experiences of victimization have an ambivalent status as candidates for narra-
> tion . . . characteristically, such experiences produce shame, anger, often guilt in
> the victim, and are regarded as secrets rather than stories to tell . . . stories about
> victimization cannot be described as interesting or remarkable without risking

academic sterility for our constructs. Nevertheless, stories told in private to co-horts are stories, and the fact that transcripts of such interactions are rarely avail-able should not justify scholarly neglect of these narratives (p. 63)

Abuse survivor narratives represent stories with such an ambivalent status, yet the important information embedded in abuse narratives makes research of such material seem not only warranted, but almost essential. Highly per-sonal and potentially risky material is often included in stories of abuse. Con-sequently, the researcher should acknowledge the potential risks and conse-quences involved for the teller of the material, and handle the narratives with care and sensitivity.

Another factor that makes the study of personal narratives difficult is the ephemeral nature of such performances. The ephemeral nature of narrative performance makes retrieval of the emotions, contexts, relationships, and so forth, quite limited. Hence, the researcher should use caution when analyzing narratives, and acknowledge that full retrieval cannot be accomplished. Fine (1984) claims, "even when we have audio and video or film recordings to pre-serve them, the sounds and images are fluid—they will not hold still for analysis" (p. 1).

Issues such as sensitivity to the other, the use of highly sensitive informa-tion, and the ephemeral nature of the material make research on personal nar-ratives problematic. However, careful attention to research design can mini-mize risks while still increasing our understanding of this sensitive topic. Geffner, Rosebaum, and Hughes (1988) contend that, "family violence re-search has evolved over the past 20 years into a legitimate filed of study" (p. 477). Yet, according to Geffner et al. (1988), the development of coherent theories is necessary to assist:

Synthesis, explain past and current findings, and help guide research in these ar-eas. Violence, whether as physical abuse, neglect, sexual abuse, or exposure to violence must be conceptualized in a synergetic fashion in order to provide the proper context for understanding the phenomena (p. 477)

Personal narratives represent a rich source of material and research area for such a "synergetic conceptualization" to occur. Cross-disciplinary interest in personal narratives demonstrates the value of personal narratives as research material.

Because of socially constructed images of victimization, research on personal narratives requires careful attention to the construction of the research question. Loseke (1992) explains that women who have been labeled "battered women" are often judged deserving of public assistance, however, "this has not helped all victimized women" (p. 154). Loseke (1992) asks, "What about the women who don't conform to these images?"(p. 155). Further, she explains that in regarding research questions on battered women, "the most frequently asked by researchers and the public is, 'Why do they stay?' unfortunately, very few social scientists have investigated the more important questions: 'Why do men batter?' 'Why do women leave?' 'What helps them stay away?' 'What can be done to help women be safe?'" (p. 15). Consequently, researchers studying domestic violence and abuse should be sure to include the voices of abused individuals themselves. Also, researchers must not construct research questions that are guided by presuppositions and/or stereotypical attitudes regarding the group under investigation. Hence, researchers of abuse survivor narratives need to examine their own motives and possible biases. Lastly, they need to assess the interests or objectives the research is designed to serve. Such consideration could facilitate a more successful research procedure for the subjects as well as an increased understanding of the other represented in the narrative.

For this study, questions regarding narrative risk and the impact of telling on the narrator accompany questions of my own motives and predispositions. That is, as a participant in this study, I examine my role as a participant-observer and my contribution to the construction or destruction of the narrative by the interviewing procedure and subsequent analysis. Perhaps more importantly, I will explore the possibility that I carry presuppositions regarding abuse survivors' experiences into each interview, which could ultimately impact my perception of the narrative discourse. In addition, I consider the influence of socially-constructed images of abuse victims and their experiences that I have previously been exposed to, including anything from direct observation to the "T.V. Movie of the Week", which can shape interpretation of the results. Rather than seeking a futile attempt at "pure objectivity," for the analysis, I acknowledge the perceptual constraints, and attempt to account for these images in the analysis.

The interview sessions are designed to place narrators in empowered positions, by allowing them to narrate those events that they believe are important for understanding their experiences. Through the use of non-directive and non-threatening questions, the interviewees can make choices regarding topic choice, direction, and the level of disclosure.

Performance as a Method of Inquiry

Because personal narratives represent discourse which often emerges from the performance of everyday life, such material lends itself to re-performance as a way of empathizing with and understanding the experiences of abuse victims. Langellier (1989) explains the important roles of performance research on personal narratives:

The personal narrative is part of the study of everyday life and the culture of everyday talk. As some scholars note, the study of personal narratives also has political implications. Studying the communication and performance of ordinary people invites researchers to listen on the margins of discourse and to give voice to muted groups in our society (p. 243)

While the discourse offered in abuse narratives may not necessarily be classified as "ordinary" merely because it reflects the experience of "ordinary people," it represents an important source of information about human communication and the performance of everyday life. Such a research endeavor raises questions regarding the performance practitioner's impact on the lives of the narrators, in addition to the performance practitioner's capability to assess the material. For example, Stucky (1993) poses the following questions: "Is this material too sensitive to explore without formal training in psychological counseling? What impact (if any) does natural performance have on the lives of the persons whose experiences become text for performance? What impact does it have in the lives of the actors?" (p. 177).

These questions represent important concerns for the performance practitioner who chooses to engage abuse survivor narratives through performance. Accountability to the other is an important ethical concern to the researcher of such material. Additional ethical concerns include the "interests" that are served through performance, the "ownership" of the narrative text, and changes in context imposed by the re-performance.

Langellier (1989) explains that "all personal narratives . . . produce a certain way of seeing the world which privileges certain interests (stories and meanings over others)" (p. 271). Because of the inevitable impact of the researcher's own voice (commentary) on the analysis of abuse narratives, the researcher may want to pay careful attention to preserving the original narrator's voice/perspective in the performance. Langellier (1989) contends "the question of existential import of narrative, what it means and whose interests it serves—cannot be assured outside its performance, where text and context, story and discourse, are given together in their concrete embodiment" (p. 270).

Hence, engaging an other's voice through performance raises important issues of ownership and obligations to the original teller's "interests." Stahl (1983) asserts that "stories 'belong' to the tellers because they are the ones responsible for recognizing in their own experiences something that is 'story worthy' and for bringing their perception of those experiences together . . . in appropriate contexts and thus creating identifiable, self-contained narratives" (p. 268–269). In addition, Stucky (1993) contends, "changes in context and purpose entailed in the re/performance of texts highlight the need for ethical responsibility in such appropriations" (p. 176).

Consequently, a performance practitioner must consider contextual factors involved in the performance and re/performance of abuse narratives as significant influences on the resulting narrative.

Conquergood (1985) suggests a "dialogical performance" stance toward the performance of other, as an ethical and moral approach. This approach is useful when performing an other's narrative. The aim of dialogical performance:

> is to bring self and other together so that they can question, debate, and challenge one another. It is the kind of performance that resists conclusions, it is intensely committed to keeping the dialogue between the performer and the text open and ongoing" (p. 9)

Such an approach aids the performance practitioner in her or his attempt to be accountable to the other. Despite any potential risks, which may accompany performance of abuse survivor narratives, performance offers a researcher an important entrance into the lived world experience of the other who is represented in the narrative.

Conquergood (1991) asserts that performative ethnography is "an embodied practice: it is an intensely sensuous way of knowing. The embodied researcher is the instrument" (p. 180). In addition, Conquergood (1991) explains:

> Performance enables the ethnographer to experience intensely some of the feelings and pain and frustrations and confusion and dignity of the natives. The empathic identification, the imaginative leap into another mind and another world, demanded by performance, is a riskier and more acute kind of participation than standard participant-observation research . . . when the ethnographer becomes performer, he or she comes closest toward entering the world of the other, while being aware simultaneously that he or she will never *be* the other (p. 154).

Similarly, in his work on American folklore, Bauman (1989) claims, "the study of performance gives us highly productive critical and reflexive perspectives on our methods and understanding what we do" (p. 181). Consequently, performing is an important method of inquiry into the life of the other who is represented in the abuse survivor narrative. Performance of the narratives offers the researcher a way of understanding the abuse victim and survivor's experience in a way that cannot be realized by means other than embodiment through performance.

Methodology

A guiding hypothesis of this project is that narrating experiences of victimization assists abuse victims in bringing positive change to their lives. In this study, I test this hypothesis and attempt to answer the research questions, which include: What role does narrative risk play in the narratives of the participants of this study? How does the telling of abuse survivor narratives impact the teller? What can we learn about highly disclosive narratives through re-performance of abuse survivor narratives? Borrowing from Langellier's (1989) and Bauman's (1983) contentions that personal narratives are influenced by the culture in which they operate, and Kerby's (1991) notion that narration is central to our communal existence, I will examine the personal narratives of abuse survivors.

The Interview Environment

This study relies on two groups of interviewees. Interviewees include clients of Haven House, a shelter for women and children who are victims of domestic violence and abuse, as well as self-selected volunteers. Haven House is located in Hammond, IN. For nearly 20 years, a ten-member board that includes individuals from various professions, including police officers, dentists, nurses and others, has run Haven House. The shelter is partially state and city funded, and also relies on outside contributions. Clients are often referred to Haven House from police, hospital, and social service representatives.

Haven House is a two-story brick home, worn and blemished from long-term use and age. The house is absorbed into a block that is lined with closely built homes in a lower class, highly populated section of Hammond. It rests in an industrial area that is primarily populated by blue-collar, steel mill workers. Consequently, clients often include working-class women from the local community.

Before entering Haven House, you confront an intercom system directed to the main office in the back of the house. Upon entering, you move through a communal living room, in which there is a sofa, oversized chairs, a television, and, on most days, several young children interacting with their mothers. The first floor of the house contains offices, the living room, a communal kitchen, and a large dining room with several tables for the clients. Mealtime is a communal experience as well. The shared cooking and cleaning responsibilities given to the clients stress the sense of community at Haven House. Upstairs, five bedrooms are available to clients, only on rare occasions when the house is full, are clients asked to share rooms with other families. At most times during the day, the house is filled not only with young children at play, but outside noises of high traffic of cars and trucks as they pass by the house.

At the time of this study, clients of the shelter could stay up to 30 days at a time when exiting abusive relationships. After three days at the shelter, the

Counseling Coordinator would assist the client in planning for continued safety and independence from the abuser, of so desired by the client. Haven House represents a neutral place, where victims of abuse can safely consider their future plans and options for survival.

Participants in the Study

The participants for this study include three African American women, one Latina woman, seven white women, and one white man. Seven of the participants are working-class individuals, five have a middle-class background. The participants ages are distributed as follows: one participant belongs in the 18–25 year-old category, three participants are 26–35 years of age, six are 36–45 years old, and two participants are 46–55 years of age.

Clients of Haven House

Participants include residents of Haven House. These interviewees include women who have recently exited abusive relationships and have sought safe housing either on their own behalf, or through the assistance of police, medical, or social workers. Residents include women who live in Northwest Indiana, including the cities of Hammond, Hobart, East Chicago, and other neighboring communities. A Counseling Coordinator for Haven House obtained the names of potential subjects for the study from interested clients who live at the shelter. After the coordinator approved our meeting, I contacted the clients who volunteered to be a part of the study. Only those individuals who are removed from abusive relationships have been interviewed.

Self-Selected Volunteers

In addition to clients of Haven House, some individuals approached me, seeking involvement in the study. These participants included students at Southern Illinois University at Carbondale. These interviewees approached me after learning of the topic of the research, and requested the inclusion of their narratives in this research.

Conducting the Interviews

Nine of the interviews for this study were conducted either on-site at Haven House or at Southern Illinois University at Carbondale. Additional interviews were conducted by telephone or in the interviewees' home or office. The interviews, which occurred at Haven House, took place in the daytime, when the house was fully staffed. The interviews occurred in the various rooms of

the house, for example, in the kitchen, the main office, the adjacent staff office, or in the living room. No interviews took place in the upstairs area,
which is reserved for the clients' personal use. Because of the time of the day
and location of the interviews, the sessions often competed with activity of
children, interruptions by other clients needing assistance, meal preparation,
and so forth. Consequently, the sessions were quite informal. Some participants interviewed with their children present, which also led to increased activity and some interruptions. The informal context seemed conducive to the
interviewees' disclosure, as they told their stories in a safe environment,
where they shared common experiences with other clients.

Four of the interviews, which involved self-selected volunteers, occurred
on-campus at Southern Illinois University at Carbondale, Illinois. The on-
campus locales included one of three conference rooms. The interviews were
conducted face-to-face in an area of the conference rooms where a sofa or a
table and chairs facilitated an informal atmosphere for the interview. An important goal for the on-campus interviews was selecting a space that would
be conducive to a private conversation, a locale in which interviewees would
not fear interruption by students, faculty, or other university personnel. The
on-campus interviews took place at a variety of times during the day. Most
occurred in the daytime, some in the evening hours.

In all of the interview sessions for this study, particular attention was given
to making the interviewees feel at ease. At the beginning of the interview sessions, interviewees were given an informed consent form to read and sign.
Next, the interviewees and I would spend time discussing the research in a bit
more depth. I assured the participants that their life stories would be handled
with caution, I stressed that their confidentiality would be preserved, and that
they could end the session at any time, if they decided to do so. Generally, the
discussions turned to casual conversation, or small talk. From there, I would
begin asking the interviewees specific questions regarding their abusive relationships. The questions were open-ended and non-directive, so that the interviewees could select the information to include which they believed to be
most relevant to the research topic. This also allowed the interviewees to
determine the level of disclosure they felt comfortable engaging during the
sessions.

I concluded the interviews with a brief summary of the topics discussed,
and asked the participants if they would like to add anything before conclud-
ing the interview sessions. The conversations then shifted to the ways in
which the interviewees could contact me for information regarding the study.
The interviews lasted approximately forty-five minutes to one and one-half
hours in length. At the close of each session, I thanked the interviewee for her
or his participation in the study, and then left the interview site.

In addition to the abuse survivors, I also interviewed three staff members of Haven House to gain more understanding of the experiences of the clients of Haven House specifically, and abuse survivors in general.

Procedure

This research required audiotaping to ensure accuracy in transcribing the narratives of the interviews. The tapes are stored in a locked file in my home. On tape, I refer to subjects by their first name only. After I transcribed the tapes, I assigned each subject a random number. After transcribing the audio taped narratives, I analyzed the data by coding for descriptions regarding the personal risk involved in the performance of abuse survivor narratives, as well as any recurrent themes that emerged from the data. Personal risk often involves deviating from standards of "appropriate" behavior imposed by societal rules and roles. By standards of appropriate behavior, I am referring to those patterns of behavior and thought that pervade a given society; those normative guidelines or scripts that are implicitly accepted by a majority of the members of a culture, and are explicitly represented in their behavior and language.

A preliminary analysis of the data collected for the study suggested the following categories of recurrent themes: traditional patriarchal roles, domestic or familial privacy, and social construction of an abuse victim. For example, traditional patriarchal roles cast members of a given biological sex into categories that promote "normative" behavioral patterns such as dominance and submission. Another standard may exist in the issue of domestic of familial privacy, which silences victims of abuse who regard issues of abuse as private rather than public matters. Behavioral standards may exist in the enculturation of thought regarding the social construction of an "abuse victim." One false notion of victimization, for example, regards the victim as the agent who is ultimately responsible for his or her own destiny, who could exit a relationship at any time, "if its was really that bad. . . ." This notion is reflected in our society's obsession with the question "Why did she stay?" Or, the notion that it victims changed their behavior, the violence would stop.

After examining the issues that emerge from the abuse survivor narratives, I conducted a close rhetorical reading of the word choice, phraseology, and position of the emergent themes within the narratives, which is used by the narrators to describe their experience. From this reading, I will discuss what has been learned about narrative risk and performance expectations, and how these factors affect the teller's experience. Additionally, I will discuss relevant issues regarding the re-performance of abuse survivor narratives through an analysis of performance knowledge generated from the stage production of *Breaking the Cycle*. This production included re-performance of abuse survivor narratives compiled from interview material, printed narratives and literature regarding domestic violence and abuse.

Research data regarding the production will include my own experiences as material gatherer and director. Other data will include experiences described by cast members who re-performed the material on stage. I will examine the material selection, performer interaction, rehearsal process, and performance of the narrative text.

Chapter Three

Coding the Narratives

CODING

The transcription and coding of the narratives were guided, to a great extent, by the work of Strauss & Corbin (1990). During the transcribing process, I made an effort to be as inclusive as possible, by transcribing the narratives in their entirety and allowing the preliminary coding scheme to emerge and eventually be refined into an accurate reflection of the data collected. Consequently, false starts, use of language fillers and so on were included in the transcribed material. Throughout the process, I made a conscious effort to be aware of meanings and contexts, so that any subjective distortion of the collected material would be kept to an absolute minimum. Above all, I sought to protect the narrator's anonymity and preserve the narrator's voice in the transcriptions. For example, names and specific identifying details such as specific places were omitted from the final transcripts so that the narrators could not be identified when the narrative excerpts were published. This was done to reduce any added risk of retribution of an abuser who might recognize the narrator in the renditions. Such omissions were handled carefully so that the narrator's voice (perspective) would remain intact, to reduce changes in context that might be imposed upon the transcribed material.

According to Straus & Corbin (1990), "coding represents the operations by which data are broken down, conceptualized, and put back together in new ways" (p. 57). For this study, I used a coding procedure which borrows from Straus and Corbin's three-step process. This process involves open coding, axial coding, and selective coding. Open coding: pertains specifically to the naming and categorizing of the phenomenon through close examination of the data

38

> . . . the data are broken down into discrete parts, closely examined, compared for similarities and differences, and questions are asked about the phenomena as reflected in the data (Straus & Corbin, 1990, p. 62.)

For this study, I examined the data on many levels, including audiencing the original telling, repeatedly listening to the audio taped interviews, transcribing the interviews, and conducting a close reading of the transcribed material. For example, as I transcribed the material, I heard many topics recur in the material generated from the interview sessions. As these topics recurred, I wrote them down for later analysis. Next, after completing the transcribing process, I printed the material, I read carefully through the stories and in the margins noted similar topics which recurred; this became a more visual part of the analysis. Many of the topics or themes recurred frequently within the narratives and across the twelve narratives I transcribed. From this coding, I was able to identify overlapping topic areas that would eventually lead to the themes of empowerment and disempowerment identified in this study. Next, I scrutinized the data using axial coding, that is:

> a set of procedures by whereby the data are put back together in new ways after open coding, making connections between categories. This is done by utilizing a coding paradigm involving conditions, context, action/interactional strategies and consequences (Straus & Corbin, 1990, p. 96)

During this step, issues of narrator stance emerged. These issues involve the positioning of the narrator in varying degrees of empowered and disempowered stances, as reflected in the narrator's word choice and topics of discussion. I analyzed these stances through assessing the context of the telling, the teller-listener interaction, and assessing the risks/consequences involved. I noted not only the words the narrators used to describe their experiences, but their demeanor in the re-telling and the contexts they described. For example, how the narrator described the role of their participation in the event or the role of their abuser, the circumstances that led them through the situation, and so on. In other words, whether they were using a more positive or negative sense of self as they described certain abusive recollections. This then lead to combining the recurring topics and the context of the retellings to define thematic consistencies in the material.

Next, I used selective coding. Selective coding, according to Straus and Corbin (1990), is "the process of selecting the core category, systematically relating it to other categories, validating those relationships and filling in categories that need further refinement and development" (p. 116). At this point in the coding, I examined the topics which were presented and discussed in the interview sessions, while simultaneously observing the context of the recountings, that is, the positioning of the participants in the stories, that positive or negative "spin" that was often placed on the excerpts generated by the study. From this selective coding process, two categories of survivor discourse emerged, including discourse of disempowerment which perpetuates silence and discourse of empowerment which facilitates change. In the next section I will discuss the themes which emerged from the selective coding. In addition, excerpts of the audio-taped narratives are included as examples of each category. At this point, it is important to note that these themes are not as dichotomous as the labels imply. The use of these themes existed on a continuum which ranged in its level of empowering or disempowering contexts. Additionally, the themes are not presented in any prioritized order. Each theme recurred frequently across the narratives collected for the study. These themes did, however, generally reflect an empowered or disempowered stance on the part of the storyteller in their perceptions reflected in the narrative discourse.

ANALYSIS

Themes of Disempowerment Which Perpetuate Silence

After coding the themes which recurred in the language of the narrators for this study, several themes of disempowerment were identified. Themes of disempowerment include the narrators' references to and/or examples of (1) traditional roles, (2) relational loyalty, (3) the social construction of abuse victims, (4) perceived power dynamics, (5) economic insecurity, (6) threat of injury or loss, (7) lack of recourse, (8) attachment to the abuser and (9) self-destructive behavior.

Traditional Roles

Traditional roles involves an individual's complacency with traditional patriarchal definitions of acceptable gender performance or portrayal, that is, their effort to fit into stereotypical gender roles. It often involves dominance and submission manifested in roles of parent, spouse, or child. Additionally, individuals who embrace traditional roles tend to idealize the traditional family unit. References to traditional roles appeared frequently in the survivors' discourse. In the following example, the narrator describes her transition from the role of daughter to wife as a move from one submissive role to the next:

> he was a lot of firsts for me, and going from daddy's house to my husband's house was the way I felt. And he was still an authority figure, like a continua-

tion of my father, even though I didn't perceive him as someone having a need to be fathered. I wasn't looking for a daddy when I married him, but just being under the rule and roof of parents, and then going from that situation, never having anything that made me autonomous, moving into an apartment with him, made me feel like, looking back, like I was still under the rule of a dominant personality. During the time I grew up, the time I was growing up, I was submissive. I would acquiesce if there was a problem. . . . So, it was not an unfamiliar role for me to play, to be submissive, to go along with what the popular rule was, and it was only popular because he was making it-his decision.

The narrator continued to describe her own feelings of frustration when her husband made the decision that she would not attend college. She explained that she felt "defenseless" against his "dominance". This narrator's account of dominance and submission represents the significance traditional patriarchal roles can have within a family structure. By "acquiescing" when problems occurred in her life, she continually reinforced her submission to more powerful individuals in her life.

Relational Loyalty

This refers to a belief that an individual is obligated to remain silent, ignore, or fail to act against abuse to protect a spouse, significant other, parent, sibling, friend, and so on, merely for the purpose of preserving the relationship they share. One example of relational loyalty is manifested in familial silence. This narrator describes his attempt to ignore the impact of the emotional abuse he and his family endured, by covering up incidents of abuse:

> there was always an air of—it was like a stand off in our house all the time. Somebody was always mad at someone else, and my dad was usually at the center of it. Like, I'd come home and find broken glass everywhere. One way I used to cope with that when I was younger, and I probably picked this up from my mom is, I used to clean. I thought I could take care of the problem if I hid it away . . . so you'd come home, and no one would know anything was wrong. All the glass was thrown away and out outside in the garbage, and pictures were neatly stacked. I used to do that a lot.

This narrator's behavior involves a failure to act against the abuse, through his attempt to cover up the abuse. With this behavior, he was preserving the nature of his relationship with his father, and in a sense, protecting his father by his inability to confront him. By hiding or covering up the abusive incidents, he was perpetuating silence, not in the absence of articulating his experience necessarily, but through the absence of a counter-action, such as confrontation or allowing the results to be seen by others. A staff member of the shelter for victims of abuse and violence explained that individuals remain silent for a number of reasons:

> There's a lot of various reasons for silence. They're silent because they're—they technically might know it's wrong, that this shouldn't be happening, and I shouldn't let anyone know that this is happening, this is happening to me. That's one thing. They're silent because they're not really sure, they're afraid that if they say something, they may have to act on it. . . . I'm gonna have to do something about it. I might have to leave.

Consequently, the resistance to take an assertive stance can perpetuate silence. Relational loyalty is often closely aligned with traditional roles. For example, a wife may remain silent regarding abuse by her husband, because she feels as a wife she has a responsibility to protect him.

Social Construction of an Abuse Victim

This category involves social construction as perceived by the abused, abuser, or other members of a given society. It occurs when an individual does not "fit" into socially accepted ideals of victimization. Consequently, the individual may not be afforded assistance as a victim of abuse. Such a construction can be disempowering to victims of abuse, by placing them in narrowly defined constructs which influence perception and behavior. Some examples include instances of victim blame, self blame, or not being validated by the system, that is, a police officer's refusal to charge the abuser or remove the abuser from the premises. A staff member at the shelter describes an example of a victim's experience, when she is asked to leave her house and go to a shelter:

> Many times, it doesn't matter that this could be their home, but the police will actually make them get up, get the children dressed, and bring them out. Saying that, instead of taking the abuser to jail . . . and make him, let him sit in jail all night, instead taking this woman from her home and the kids. A lot of women find that frustrating.

By removing the victim, the officer's behavior appears to be that of "punishing" the victim, and "rewarding" the abuser, by allowing him to remain in his home. One survivor describes how she felt when she believed the legal system failed to recognize her victimization:

> I was trying to get them to see that I'm not crazy, and I'm not losing it, I'm just hurt. I don't have no family, I don't have any friends. I don't know where to turn. . . . I felt lost. I felt like society had turned their back on me. I felt like. . . . I

could die tomorrow and they would throw me in a box and just say, "she wasn't a good mother anyway. She was lost. There was nothing we could do for her".

Even in the recountings by the staff of the shelter regarding their screening process, the staff alluded to their *ability* to gauge an individual's eligibility for entrance into the shelter, remarking that most of the time, "it's not that hard actually, it gets better with time". This suggests that the staff, as well as others, have a preconceived image or "standard" which defines what an abuse victim looks like or sounds like, thus reinforcing stereotypes.

Perceived Power Dynamics

This category includes institutional or personal levels of perceived power that can limit the victim's ability to engage in assertive behavior, leave abusive relationships, or narrate experiences. The power dynamics may involve issues of race, class, gender, and so on. The individual often has low self esteem, is isolated from others, and is demeaned by the abuser. One way perceived power dynamics is reinforced on a personal level is through physical force. This narrator describes his fear of his father's physical power:

> he came and slammed me against the wall, and I was just yelling, "shit," and threw me down the stairs and I wasn't gonna fight back, cause he's like 280, big guy, and I have no power against him. . . . I knew that if I swung and hit him, he would hit me three times as hard. So, I just took it. And, he hit me in the face once or twice . . . it kinda hurt but it was no big deal, I've been hurt ten times worse.

Later, he recounted another incident in which he felt powerless:

> I heard the screaming in the basement once again. My mom was down there, she was trying to console him. She was like so petrified of what he was going to do, or how he was going to act about it. And I heard him scream at her . . . and dicing her to pieces, and my mom was a fragile person sometimes. She's hardened up. She was crying and that, and she just gave up and went upstairs, and I heard her crying in the living room. I can't stand hearing my mom cry, just being her son. Now, I'm taking this protective type attitude and I came down and told her I was sorry, and she said she was sorry and she couldn't talk to him. He get's so angry. And we sat there and held each other for a while, and I was so furious at my father for doing that to her.

In the above passages, the narrator begins explaining the power dynamics which occurred in the hierarchy of his family structure. He alludes to his father's ability to reduce his mother's self-esteem, by "dicing her to pieces," however, he also speaks of his emergence as his mother's "protector." While this could be understood as yet another example of perceived power or traditional roles in the mother is a female who could be "protected" by her male son, the narrator describes his behavior differently than he labels it. He explains that he comforted and held his mother. This behavior highlights alternative roles (which will be discussed in the next section) that he assumed during this time, possibly the role of protector, but more likely, the role of comforter or friend or ally against their mutual abuser.

Other incidents of perceived power can be asserted through emotional control. Another survivor explains her sense of isolation and fear:

> here I was secluded way back in these woods, and, you know, it was scary to me. I I just kind of stayed to myself. I didn't go places, I was, just kind of not allowed to drive, have friends over, talk on the telephone. I mean, these were almost like unstated rules. He would show his, his indignation to those kinds of things, you know, kind of forceful walking around, and that kind of thing.

Additionally, power dynamics can be promoted by outside institutions. In the following example, a narrator explains her difficulty in finding a place to live:

> They have public housing, but they have such a waiting list for public housing, that it's hard to get into a, what they would call a project. And then, that's another situation, cause you really don't want your kids brought up in the projects because it's so hard core. You know, society already has them labeled. It's the children we don't want, which makes it very hard on them from the beginning. If you take a look at Cabrini Green, they have their own police force. You know, they're fenced in and which means society is telling them, "you're not good enough to be out here, and what we have around here, you're just—you're just a ghetto baby".

Institutional power over finances, housing, societal value systems, and so forth, can make abuse victims feel disempowered, and can contribute to their belief that they are powerless and cannot exit abusive relationships.

Economic Insecurity

This exists when a victim of abuse remains in an abusive situation because of financial dependence on the abuser. There were references to economic insecurity in all of the narratives collected for this study. Many alluded to a fear of not being able to support themselves, their children, their home. The staff narratives often alluded to the financial constraints which victims face. One staff narrator explains:

> They feel they can't make it on their own. . . . If you have a husband who's working and supporting you, regardless of how he's treating you, and your chil-

dren are getting the things they need, and that maybe other children have, what are you going to do? How are you gonna provide for them? You get support. What is the maximum you get, fifty dollars a week for a child . . . how are you gonna support yourself if you've never had any training, if you don't have job skills, or if you have children young enough that you wouldn't be able to work because then you have to find child care. And, you weren't going to make enough money to pay for the child care.

Economic insecurity is often intensified by the abuser's controlling behavior. Victims are often isolated, unable to work outside the home or to develop job skills. Consequently, leaving their abuser becomes even more difficult. One client of Haven House describes the financial difficulties she faces:

I have been on the phone calling about apartments. Nobody wants to rent me an apartment. I look for one bedroom, they want three and four hundred dollars, they want a security deposit. It's at least seven hundred dollars to move in. And where am I going to get seven hundred dollars? I don't have any family I can run to and say, loan me this money. And when you do go to them and tell them, well I get an AFDC check that is 229 dollars a month, they're like, you can't afford this, and we don't want to take no trustee. So, the financial situation is what makes it really hard, it does. I mean, it helps, the money the government gives me, Lord knows it helps. But, it's just not enough. There's nothing I can do with it.

As reflected in the above quote, an individual's socio-economic class can influence the options that are available to them and their family. Without the ability to provide for themselves and their dependents, victims may not be *able* to leave their abusive partners. Economic insecurity affects the lives of victims in two significant ways. First, it can create tension between the abuser and the victim which leads to abuse. Secondly, economic insecurity makes escape from abusive relationships more difficult.

Threat of Injury or Loss

This includes a belief that acting on one's own behalf, engaging in highly personal disclosure, or trying to leave an abusive relationship could result in injury, death, loss of children, loss of status, home, and so on. Threat of injury or death can make it nearly impossible for a victim of abuse to confidently leave an abusive relationship. One survivor explains how she felt when she sought help from law enforcement and legal service providers:

I went to see that attorney a couple of days later. I was so frightened that he would see me, that I couldn't go and make a police report. I was afraid that he might see me go into the police station, so I didn't make a police report until about a week later. I did go and tell them about it, so that I'd have something on record. I didn't receive any treatment at that time, even thought I was having a lot of headaches, probably mostly because of the tension that was in the house. And, when I saw this attorney. . . . I went any side road I could to get to his office to try to avoid being seen. I was so paranoid at that point, that I was afraid that he'd see me, and take the kids, or beat me again.

Another survivor explains how her abuser threatened her life by describing how he had allegedly killed someone else:

the next time I saw him, which was a few days later, he was crying, he was shaking, he was drunk, and he said he killed a man. And he gave me every gory detail. And then he looked at me and said, "if I can kill him, I can surely kill you—you'd better think about what it is you do next" . . . I was f—ing frantic. I was dizzy. I was scared. I thought I just couldn't, I didn't know what to do. I was petrified.

Lack of Recourse

This category represents abused individuals' feelings that they have no recourse (based on a variety of constraints) and consequently, remain complacent or silent regarding the abuse. The individuals feel hopeless, that they cannot make it on their own. One survivor explains that she felt she had no recourse because of her abuser's continual demeaning of her:

all through this he would tell me, I, I—you know, his favorite line would be something like, "you can't wipe your ass. How do you expect to make it in this world? You need me. You cannot make it without me." And I bought into this, and I guess, you know, over years of just being very complacent, and very dependent on him. It was really easy to buy into that . . . I can't do anything without him.

Being controlled by their abusers, not only leaves the victim with feelings of hopelessness, with no avenues of recourse, but is closely aligned with perceived power dynamics and traditional roles, where the abuser has control over the behavior, thoughts, and emotions of their victims.

Attachment to the Abuser

In this category, the individual is drawn to the abuser because of love, the abuser's need for nurturing, the abuser's personality, or a belief that the abuser will change. This attachment can also include infatuation, obsession, excitement of the relationship, or co-dependency on drugs or alcohol. One survivor explained:

I don't know, I don't know—it's got to be habit, just a habit. I'm so, you know he's been there since I was fifteen years old. I'm, thirty now, okay, . . . and I don't know, I just don't know why I stayed with him. It's just something I can't—if he wasn't there, I missed him. But when he beat me up, I hated him. You know there were two sides to my husband, that alcoholic side and the drugs and there was him being sober. And, I guess that was what I was holding on to. . . . I kept thinking, well, he's gonna change, he's gonna change.

Many abuse victims hold onto the belief that their abuser will change. A staff member explains how this belief can keep them in a life of abuse:

She wants to believe him. She thinks maybe he won't do this again. I want to give him one more chance. I can't see myself living on Welfare. I don't want to raise my children in government homes, you know, things like that. Or, "he's really good with the kids." They find excuses to help them believe that he's never going to do that again.

The belief that the abuser will change coupled with constraints of an uncertain future, economic insecurity and so forth, can keep a victim in an abusive relationship indefinitely.

Self-destructive Behavior

This occurs when an abuse victim's feelings of hate, anger, or hopelessness lead to negative personal behavior by the victim, which can result in physical or emotional injury to the victim, i.e., abuse of alcohol, drugs, eating disorders. One survivor reported:

It got really crazy, one time we were, we were in a fight. He told me, "go sit in the kitchen, I don't want to look at your face anymore." And I was in the kitchen screaming obscenities, "screw you, shut up." I got up, walked over to the kitchen drawer, "what are you doing?" "I went to get a cigarette." "Sit your ass down." "Yeah, Okay." And I cut my wrist, lit up a cigarette, and got quiet. . . . I was bleeding all over the place.

In the next excerpt, the speaker explains how her feelings of lack of recourse against her abuser's dominance led to self-destructive behavior on her part:

and then all of a sudden, I get up one morning, and he's gone. And, I'm like, this isn't right. Now see what he did was, he just worked it in perfectly so he had joint custody too, so I couldn't say anything about him leaving. So, when he left, he had contacted his attorney, and told his attorney that I was, I wasn't stable, and that they thought I was headed for a nervous breakdown and some other things, and he got a signed statement from the doctor that said he thought I was headed for a nervous breakdown. So, then the court gave him full custody of my kids. So, I battled with that for a long time. After I lost my kids, then I had just given up, and I went to drinking and doing drugs and everything, which landed me in prison. I went to prison for three years and seven months. And, the whole time I was in prison, I was thinking about, God, I have never really done anything to hurt anybody, why am I suffering so much? I'm a good mother, a good wife. I worked hard. I never stole from anybody. I don't lie to anybody. What's wrong? You know? And, my situation was going pretty much, I was at the wrong place at the wrong time.

During the interviews, survivors described co-dependency on alcohol and drugs, prostitution, and other self-destructive behaviors, that they believe were at least to some degree, a result of the abusive homes in which they lived. Their accounts represent some of the ways that abuse victims become self-destructive, in an effort to cope with or end abuse. By becoming co-dependent on drugs or physically injuring themselves, the survivors "punished" or hurt themselves, just as their abusers had hurt them.

Themes of disempowerment, as reflected in the language of the abuse survivors, are often related to a positioning of the narrator in the story, their stance. For example, when the narrators assume traditional roles or conform to the perceived power dynamics imposed on them by their abusers, their stance has been reduced to a secondary position. They are disempowered by the dominance the abuser claims over their behavior. Additionally, when victims of abuse believe they are responsible for the abuse because they don't conform to socially constructed ideals of a victimized individual, they are assuming a disempowered stance.

Attitudes of disempowerment, such as feeling of lack of recourse or attachment to the abuser can position the victims in powerless roles of complacency with the abuse. They may believe that they are unable to assume an assertive stance for fear that they will lose the abused individual they are drawn to. Economic insecurity is a pragmatic constraint that casts victims in varying degrees of disempowered stances. Self-destructive behavior is perhaps one of the most debilitating of the disempowering stances. Emergence from disempowered position requires a victim to engage in increasingly empowered stances. These stances, or issues of narrator positioning, were reflected in the themes of empowerment.

Themes of Empowerment Which Can Facilitate Change

In contrast to the themes of disempowerment I described in the previous section, the final coding yielded the following themes of empowerment: (1) responsibility to dependents, (2) support of a social network, (3) reconceptualization of the experience by the survivor, (4) assessing the costs of the relationship, (5) personal achievement, (6) confronting uncertainty, (7) rejecting constraints and (8) emphasizing alternative roles.

Responsibility to Dependents

This occurs when the victim begins to view his or her obligation to children/dependents as more significant than the costs of leaving the relationship (not inconsistent with traditional roles). One survivor stated:

> He hit me repeatedly and the kids ran out of the house. I was getting ready to take them to school, they ran out of the house and were hitting his legs and crying and screaming for him to stop.

Later, in the interview, the same narrator continued:

> The real deciding factor for me was that day in January when he was beating me and my kids were beating on him, and crying for him to stop. It suddenly hit me, it sounds bizarre—this bolt of lightning, this revelation—my God, what am I doing to my kids? By taking this, I'm teaching my daughter that this is the way you should be treated by men, and you should accept this. And my sons, I feel that they were learning to mimic their father's behavior, to become—they would have the potential to become wife beaters, or at least abusing—being abusive, and that was the deciding factor.

Despite the fear which had previously kept this woman from leaving her abusive husband, this narrator's sense of her responsibility to her children became more significant and led her to take a more assertive stance and leave her abusive mate. When I asked a staff member at the shelter what helps a victim leave, her quick response was, "the children". She explained that often the abuse escalates to the children, and while victims may continually tolerate abuse against themselves, they are often moved to action in order to protect their children.

Reconceptualization of the Experience

This involves a shifting of the blame away from the victim. The victims begin to view themselves as having more self-worth. They recognize that the abusers are victimizing them and that victimization cannot be controlled by altering the victims' behaviors.

In some respects, the narrative act itself can be an articulated reconceptualization of the narrator's experience, in that, the narrators select details, choose material to include, position themselves in certain ways, and so forth,

during the telling. Yet, for this category, the narrators were coded as reconceptualizing the experience in moments of the narration where they became
self-reflexive, reexamined their original feelings, and commented upon them.
One survivor describes her spouse's abusive tendencies, and his reaction to
her leaving him:

> He beat me because he could not give up the control he had over me, he couldn't
> tolerate the fact that he could no longer dominate or control me. He tried scar-
> ing me, he would get drunk and make threats to me, and he did everything he
> could possibly do to intimidate me, and though many times I was intimidated,
> and I was afraid, once I left, he—that hold was broken.

This account demonstrates how a survivor, once removed from the control of
the abuser, can reflect upon the origins of the abuse. In this example, the survivor recognizes that the responsibility for the abuser lies with her abuser, not
her own behavior. Hence, she can reconceptualize the abuse by shifting blame
away from herself as victim to her husband's abusive actions. Another narrator recounted her move to survivorship:

> I didn't want anybody to know what he was doing. I wanted to let them think
> our relationship was going so good, we didn't have want for nothing. But inside
> I was dying, dying—wanted to kill myself, maybe things would be better if I
> wasn't alive. And I thought about the kids, that stopped me. I ain't gonna say
> right now my world revolves around my kids, but it's now—I do care about my-
> self. I had to learn, hey, you're not a bad person—you're a good person. I'm
> what they call a survivor—and I'm gonna survive. I don't need a man to tell me
> this.

This quote marks a transitory point for this narrator. She explains how she
moved from silence about her abuse, which left her with thoughts of suicide,
to a more empowered position as a person who defines herself as a survivor.
This excerpt marks a period when this survivor, who had just recently removed herself from her abusive marriage, labels herself a survivor. The articulated re/expression of her desire and belief that she will "survive," emphasizes the transitory power of projecting a positive future story on
facilitating such a change. By eventually telling others about the abuse, this
narrator was able to break the pretense surrounding her marriage, that is, to
stop covering up the abuse, and receive help from a social network. Although
she was only recently separated from her abuser at the time of this telling, she
envisions herself not as a victim, but a survivor. This envisioning is facilitated
by the narrative act. It was through personal narration that she gained access
to the shelter. It was through narration that she is encouraged by the staff and
able to work through some of her personal thoughts and feelings about her

abuse, and plan for her future. As Jean-Paul Sartre wrote, "each one, by re-inventing his own issue, invents himself. Man must be invented each day" (p. 3). Through each presentation of their personal stories of abuse, these narrators actively re-invent themselves. Using the narrative act is an import way in which the narrators set the stage for recollections of past triumphs over adversity, as well as setting goals for their future.

Support of a Social Network

This category includes availability of financial or personal (i.e., emotional) support of family, friends, institutions, who may provide a place to go, legal representation or other assistance. These types of references were mentioned quite frequently by survivors. Many alluded to the importance of being believed and aided by family, friends, and support services in facilitating their escape from abusive relationships. The lack of support of a social network often leaves a victim feeling significantly alone and disempowered. A survivor describes her pain when her friend sided with her abuser, as a response to negative behavior by the survivor:

> He's got something about him where people just, I don't know, even my best friend turned on me to stick up for him, and that hurt. "Well, hey, go home and take your beating," she tells me. I said, "are you crazy? That man will kill me." But she said, "you did something wrong, you stayed out, you ain't supposed to do that." I said, "That's it." "And my husband said that he didn't want you here."

This blatant lack of support was very disempowering to this victim. Although she also believed that her behavior was inappropriate, she didn't believe that she deserved to be beaten in order to return home. She added, "I found out, don't trust anyone. I found out the hard way." The absence of a support network may leave a victim believing that there is no recourse. However, support services and emotional support are significant factors which can aide the victim's transition from a life of abuse to a life of survivorship.

Assessing the Costs of the Relationship

When assessing the costs, the individual recognizes the potential risks of remaining in the relationship, that is, personal injury or death, and determines that the risks of staying in the relationship are just as significant or more significant than leaving the relationship. In the following excerpt, one survivor describes how she decided to leave. She had been in prison and came back to her abuser for a short time:

> I learned so much. I've been out maybe now, I was telling them about five months now, and I've already gotten beat maybe twice in four months. What

you got to beat me for? . . . He's changed worse in these last two years for the worse, and realize that . . . I put up with your stuff here, now, for four months and you would kill me already. But that's how I ended up leaving him and coming here.

This excerpt reflects the narrator's perception that remaining in the abusive relationship was potentially as dangerous as exiting the relationship, and therefore, she chose to leave. While this may appear disempowering upon first glance, it reflects a shift in this narrator's way of thinking. It reflects her perception that she was able to take the risk, preserve her life and bring about a positive change.

A staff member at the shelter explains how they try to convince clients to assess the costs of their relationships, by examining the seemingly inevitable escalation of violence. She says when they finally begin to assess the costs of staying:

They learn to accept that he's not going to change, the violence won't stop. I'm not going to put up with it anymore, and usually, they will leave the relationship. But usually, it takes like the children or maybe they went to the hospital and they realized how close to death I was this time, and what's gonna stop him the next time? And that's part of the fear, the fear that he will kill. It's fear and strength all at the same time. But it gives you finally, the strength.

Personal Achievement

This includes a belief that the future holds hope. This is implied in projections of positive plans for the future, i.e., getting a job, going to school, increase in self confidence, and so forth. One narrator explains how her life has changed:

we have a better relationship now, and at times, I can enjoy his company, now. Because I know I can shut the door, I don't have to answer the phone. I don't have to be afraid, because I can pick up the phone and call my detective, I can call my attorney. And even though he doesn't seem to be affected by these things, I think he knows the ball is in my court. And, I feel, though I don't want to abuse this, I don't feel any superficial pride or glory in having this power, except that it has made me free of him. I don't try to abuse the power I have, because I never wanted to control him, I never wanted to dominate his life, all I ever wanted to have was—what I wanted to do was go to school, and to have children, and to have a good, decent home life.

This quote demonstrates this narrator's feelings of personal achievement, for example, in her ability to take control over the relationship, and finally fulfill her personal goals.

Confronting Uncertainty

This involves the struggle between hope and doubt. Even though the survivors have taken steps to secure independent futures, they experience feelings of uncertainty regarding their ability to make it. Overcoming uncertainty can include confronting societal constraints which produce uncertainty, that is, the individual's perceived importance within a given society. This category is similar to lack of recourse, but usually results in positive actions toward independence from the abuser. The following excerpt recounts one narrator's feelings of uncertainty regarding the future of her and her baby, after she had to leave everything, and is now trying to build a life from next to nothing:

> I ended up losing everything. I left my apartment. I left everything in it, and I just said, "hey, piss on it, I'm through, I'm really through." And it's a very scary feeling, it really is, to wonder, you know, I always wonder, are things gonna get easier? What do I have to do to make it easier on my little girl? . . . sometimes it's hard to lay down at night and just be by yourself. I mean, at first, the peace of mind is wonderful, and the solitude is wonderful. And then, it gets old after a while, and you start getting lonely and you realize, it's just me. Shit. This is my family right here, me and my baby, there's nobody else.

The ability to confront uncertainty is a significant challenge to a victim who attempts to transcend into an empowered, independent way of life.

Emphasizing Alternative Roles

Like compensation, the survivors try to highlight alternative roles in their own repertoire of behavior which are distinct from the roles of victimization they share with their abuser, when they emphasize alternative roles. This often involves a reconceptualization of self, that is, emphasizing the role of mother, a strong individual, and so forth. One survivor describes her alternative role as head of her household, that is, she now has the ability to stand up for herself and choose whether or not her ex-husband can be in her home:

> It's like nothing else that you could imagine. It's probably like being—it's truly liberation, to know that even though you have to be subject to some of the things they want to say—the nasty things, that for the first time you can really stand up and say what you want to say, you can kick him out of the house. You know, the house is now mine. It's my house, you have no right to come here and say anything abusive to me, if I don't like you for any reason, you have to get out.

Not only does she highlight her new role of independence and strength, she later expresses her plans for the future:

> I feel like there is hope for the future, when I get up in the morning . . . I feel like I've got a purpose, I belong to myself. And, by belonging to myself, and trying to be all that I can be, trying to use my potential to the max, that I can be a better mother to my kids.

Similar accounts by other narrators demonstrated the importance of highlighting alternative roles in the victim's transition to the role of survivor. Whether it was the role of mother, student, or protectors, these narrators chose to emphasize these roles over past roles of victimization in their references to future plans.

Rejecting Constraints

Similar to confronting uncertainty, the individual rejects constraints which are perceived to be imposed upon members of a given society. This can include financial or legal limitations, or value-laden constructs which can limit a victim's transcendence to survivorship. One narrator explains how she stood up for herself in court and won back joint custody of her children, who had been previously taken from her:

> So I just went back to court against him and the judge gave us joint custody. Because I just went in and told the judge, "look, I'm not no bad girl. This is what happened and I'm sorry about it".

By admitting past mistakes, which include drug use and prison time, she rejected the constraints which are often imposed upon members of a society who have not necessarily portrayed "acceptable" idealized roles of wife and mother.

Another narrator explains how she hopes to prepare her children to guard against societal expectations of traditional roles, which she believes led to her dependence on her abuser:

> I don't want to see them fall into the trap of marrying because they feel that they have to because of pressures from society, or pressure from their father's culture. I want them to know that they have to strive for self actualization and know who they really are as individuals before giving themselves to another person. . . . I want them to get their education and complete that, and I want nothing to stand in the way of that. I think that's important, especially with the kind of society . . . we live in.

This narrator's belief in education and alternative roles stems, in part, from her own inability to self actualize (resist constraints) in her marriage. She told me that she had married young, gave up dreams of going to school, and lived under the control of her abuser for fifteen years.

By overcoming constraints such as value-laden constructs, limited education (in a society that emphasizes the importance of education), the constraints embedded in the promotion of traditional roles and so forth, victims are positioned as empowered, which can assist them in their transcendence to survivorship.

Themes of empowerment involve a positioning of the narrator which is indicative of the stance the narrator assumes. While themes of disempowerment can make an individual remain silent regarding their abuse, themes of empowerment can involve a stance which facilitates change in a survivor's life. Reconceptualizing their experiences or assessing the costs of a relationship can allow a survivor to imagine alternative behavioral possibilities. Such possibilities are often prompted by the survivor's sense of responsibility to their dependents.

Realizing alternative possibilities can require support of a social network and confronting uncertainty as the survivor engages in empowered behavioral acts, such as leaving a relationship, while risking the threat of injury or loss. By rejecting the constraints they must face to become survivors, the survivors are able to emphasize alternative roles and realize personal achievement. Hence, the themes of empowerment embedded in the language of the narratives reflect alternative stances the narrators invoked to move from victimization and survivorship.

DISCUSSION

When we examine the themes which emerged from this study, it seems that telling survivor stories impacted the lives of these tellers in significant ways. Interestingly, yet not surprisingly, the rhetoric collected for this study yielded results consistent with research on domestic violence and abuse, as well as narrative studies.

Consistencies Found with Research on Domestic Violence

Many of the themes of disempowerment which recurred in the narratives collected for this study are closely aligned with past research on domestic violence and abuse. This research has generally centered on three main issues: conformity to roles, a sense of false hope that the abuser will change, and the social construction of victimization.

Conformity to Roles

Hutchings (1988) contends that societal roles place a woman in "a secondary position and causes her to devalue herself" (p. 21). This notion was reinforced in the narrators' references to traditional roles and perceived power dynamics within their abusive relationships. As Alexander, Moore and Alexander (1991) explain, abusive men generally hold "more traditional views about women than do non-abusive men" (p. 658). Often, the narrators included in this study used language which not only referenced traditional roles, but seemed to reinforce acceptance of these roles as well. For example, one narrator claimed that she was not "a bad girl." Another narrator indicated that she believed that she couldn't make it on her own, that is, without the help of her abusive male partner. Similarly, even when the narrators described alternative roles, which they considered positive for future plans, the roles were often consistent with culturally-defined, gender-specific performance expectations for a female in our society, for example, a mother protecting her child.

False Hope

Another consistency with past research on domestic violence and abuse that emerged in this study, is references to a victim's belief that the abuser will change. Hoff (1990) contends that without the ability to communicate her experience to others, a victim of abuse may harbour "wishes for reconciliation based more on fantasy than reality" (p. 175). Attachment to the abuser, relational loyalty, and lack of recourse can manifest similar wishful thinking for victims involved in abusive relationships. For example, a victim may "harbour" an unwarranted belief that the abuser will somehow change. Such a belief can result from abuse victims' sense of hopelessness or their failure to see alternative behavioral choices available to them, such as leaving the abusive situation and/or becoming independent of the abuser. Because they feel unable to change the situation and they need to believe the abuse will stop, they may fantasize about positive future behavior by the abuser.

Social Constructs of Victimization

In her description of the social construction of victimization, Loseke (1992) explains the "ideal type" of a battered woman. This "ideal" suggests that battered women are traditionally wives or mothers who are trapped, emotionally confused, isolated, overwhelmingly fearful, and suffering from physical and emotional illnesses. Many of the narratives collected for this study reflected the narrators' problems overcoming socially constructed norms of victimization and abuse. For example, every narrative collected for this study included at least one reference to the narrators' attempts to convince others that they weren't "crazy" or "insane" or "paranoid," but were truly experiencing abuse. Often, the victims were not validated as abuse victims because they did not fit the socially constructed ideals regarding abuse. However, many of the socially constructed images regarding abuse described by Loseke (1992) were alluded to in the narratives, for example, many of the narrators described their economic insecurity, their dependence on the abuser, their sense of fear and/or confusion, and so forth.

Consistencies Found with Research on Personal Narratives

Themes of empowerment that emerged from the survivor narratives collected for this study are closely aligned with past research on personal narration, including research on the "future story," context, persuasion and believability.

Future Story

Richardson (1990) claims that narration allows us to "alter the direction of our lives" (p. 117). Similarly, Polkinghorne (1988) explains the telling of narratives allows for the creation of a "future story." Consequently, for narrators involved in this study, references to personal achievement and future responsibility to dependents, became projections of their "future story." In addition, at times when the narrators engaged in reconceptualization of the experience, they were contributing to their "unfolding story" (Polkinghorne, 1988, p. 150), and engaging in reflexive activity which Turner (1981) explains, can produce "experiential knowledge" gained through the narrative event (p. 163). This reflexive activity is similar to Richardson's (1990) description of narration, that "telling one's story gives meaning to the past from the point of view of the present and future" (p. 126). Similarly, NiCarthy (1987) suggests that when victims leave their abusive mates, some seem to "experience a sudden breakthrough, similar to the 'snapping out' phenomenon in which people 'suddenly' come out of a trance-like state induced by some religious cults" (p. 310). Results of this study indicate that the narrative act can serve as a reflection of this breakthrough, as a survivor begins to project images of alternative roles which distinguish them from their past roles of victimization.

Context

Research on personal narratives demonstrates the importance of context in the telling of personal stories. Bauman (1986) explains that participants' roles and identities, rules, norms of performance, and so forth, influence the telling of personal stories. Peterson and Langellier (1997) contend that "the challenge to investigate the production of personal narrative itself requires that we take seriously the study of context—both contiguous discourse and distant constraints on text—and how one locates a boundary constituting text and context" (p. 136). This is evidenced in the narratives collected for this study, which contain multiple examples of relational loyalty and/or lack of support of a social network, which placed individuals in years of silence. One narrator chose not to narrate her story for years, to protect her listeners from their own potential reactions to the abuse. Other narrators disclosed that in the past they felt unable to tell their experience due to the absence of supportive listeners, for example, "I was never close to my family," or "even my best friend turned on me." Consequently, the context in these cases and the participants roles and identities, did not facilitate an atmosphere conducive to telling an abuse narrative.

Persuasion and Believability

Plummer (1995) suggests that "stories help organize the flow of interaction, bringing together or disrupting the relation of self to other and community" (p. 174). Further, Lucaites and Condit (1983) explain that narrators select details to include in their narratives that "make it persuasive to a specific audience" (p. 95). However, as Alcoff and Gray (1993) warn in their research on survivor discourse, "as survivors we do not need authoritative mediation of our experiences for public consumption or for experiential validation" (p. 284). Hence, the survivor/narrator must create their own validation to move increasingly toward empowered stances. When abuse victims begin to reassess the costs of the relationships, the victims scrutinize specific details of their own experience, and sometimes persuade themselves to leave the relationship that is, in audiencing their own perception of their life stories, they may begin to see their experiences differently and act to bring about change in their lives. Further, this assessment may become a significant part of their positive future discourse as it did for the narrators in this study, indicating the empowered positions they currently hold. In his discussion of personal narratives gathered from those who experience physical illness, Frank (1995) writes, "one of our most difficult duties as human beings is to listen to the voices of those who suffer" (p.25). While difficult, these interactions are vital for steps we must take to promote an end to familial violence. Such a notion *requires* researchers of personal narration to further explore the significance of storytelling of survivor discourse and change.

NiCarthy (1987) claims that while admitting that you have been abused by someone you "love or need" can be quite difficult, it can also be "the beginning of your best protection," (p. 296) in coping with what happened. Consequently, those narrators who reported a sense of personal achievement in their ability to tell others of their experience, as well as those who referenced confronting uncertainties which they encountered when leaving their abusive mates, were able to make a move toward transcendence to survivorship. That is, their ability to narrate their experience to others contributed to taking that first step.

The consistencies described in the above section are significant, in that, they demonstrate how commonalities exist across the narrative experiences of abuse survivors who include a diverse group of individuals, representing different cultural, economic, and educational backgrounds, as well as living various stages of empowerment from their abused past. Although each interviewee shared unique stories and experiences, their stories functioned for them in similar ways. The stories offered opportunities to describe their experiences in a way that facilitated not only the listener's understanding, but their own understanding as well. They used the narrative act to achieve a greater degree of sense making of who they are and how their life stories "fit" into their self-constructed identity. I was approached by someone during the course of this study and I was asked, how do you know that the interviewees are telling you the truth? My response was that there was no test or measurement used to analyze truth-telling on their part, but what seems more significant are the ways in which they constructed their perceptions of their experiences into credible stories. Herrnstein-Smith (1981) explains that narrators construct "versions" of stories based on the motives and interests such selections can serve:

> For any given narrative, there is always multiple basic stories that can be constructed in response to it because basic-ness is always arrived at by the exercise of some set of operations, in accord with some set of principles, that reflect some set of interests, all of which are, by nature variable and thus multiple. . . . The form and features of any "version" of a narrative will be a function of, among other things, the particular motives that elicited it and the particular interests and functions it was designed to serve (p. 217).

Similarly, Kerby (1991) suggests that narrative is "unavoidably selective." Lucaites and Condit (1983) explain that "in rhetorical discourse, the narrator must select and integrate only those elements of a story that make it persuasive to a specific audience" (p.95). Further, Langellier (1989) maintains:

> In narratives of personal experience, the narrative event emphasizes the personal as it features a first-person narrator . . . relating an experience from his or her perspective. The narrated event highlights the experience because the event it retells is from the teller's own life. The effect of telling a personal narrative is to enhance experience as expressivity exceeds referentiality to create a possible world (p. 255).

The abuse survivors represented in this study constructed their narrative "versions" to facilitate narrative sense making and teller empowerment. Alcoff and Gray (1993) contend a survivor must create his or her own validating experiences. This is consistent with narrative research that indicates a need to position oneself in believable roles (Lucaites and Condit, 1983; Plummer, 1995), by selecting effective narrative versions based on the audience of the narrative (Herrnstein-Smith, 1981; Kerby, 1991; Lucaites and Condit, 1983) and creating one's own "possible world" (Langellier, 1999). As I examined the narratives collected for this study, I found that the survivors used the narrative event to "create a possible world," by positioning themselves in varying degrees of empowered stances during their recountings. Through effective narration, the participants were able to gain access to a shelter, support from family and friends, and achieve personal empowerment through personal reflection. The inability to communicate their stories to others leaves those trapped in silence with little recourse, with little assistance to emerge from abusive relationships. If victims of abuse are unable to share their stories of abuse, if they are unable to name their experiences of victimization to themselves or others, they will be unable to move to empowered positions. While narration is by no means the only way in which victims of abuse move to survivorship, they cannot fully rid themselves, it appears, without coming to terms with their past roles of victimization. By acknowledging their victimization through the narrative act, victims are also able to recast themselves, metaphorically speaking, into powerful independent "roles".

Chapter Four

Personal Narratives and Change

Survivors of abuse use the performative act of storytelling to bring about change in their lives. To gain an understanding of how survivors use the narrative event, I conducted a close rhetorical reading of the narratives collected for this study. As described in Chapter Three, coding the survivor narratives yielded two primary categories of emergent themes embedded in the language of the survivor stories. These include themes of disempowerment which can perpetuate silence, and themes of empowerment which can facilitate change in the lives of abuse survivors. Themes of disempowerment include traditional roles, relational loyalty, social construction of an abuse victim, perceived power dynamics, economic insecurity, threat of injury or loss, lack of recourse, attachment to the abuser, and self destructive behavior. Themes of empowerment include responsibility to dependents, support of a social network, reconceptualization of the experience, assessing the costs of the relationship, personal achievement, confronting uncertainty, rejecting constraints, and emphasizing alternative roles. Upon close examination of the survivor narratives, I found that abuse survivors use narrative sensemaking and performative strategies to facilitate change in their lives. In the following section, I will discuss the ways in which survivors use narrative sensemaking to bring change to their lives.

NARRATIVE SENSEMAKING

Narrative sensemaking refers to the narrator's attempt to understand his or her experience more fully by engaging the act of telling. Bochner (2001) writes that narrative serves an important function of sense making in our lives, he contends, "the call of stories thus inspires us to find language that is adequate to the darkness and obscurity of experience. We narrate to make sense of ourselves and our experiences over the course of time" (p. 154). To discern the ways in which survivors make sense of their narrative recountings, I examined the following questions: What characterizes the discourse abuse survivors use in their narrative recountings? How do they use the themes of disempowerment and empowerment in their narratives? And, What is the nature or quality of the discourse survivors use in storytelling?

SURVIVOR DISCOURSE

To understand how abuse survivors use discourse in their narratives, I examine the recit, or the manner by which the narrators compose their stories. In her work on personal narratives, Herrnstein Smith (1981) describes a structuralist view of narrative which asserts that every narrative has at least two parts. These parts, or dualisms embraced by some narrantologists, are expressed in what Herrnstein Smith (1981) labels doublet terms, such as the "signified" and "signifier," "content plane" and "expression plane," "histoire" and "recit," and so forth. In her discussion of Chatman's (1978) work on narrative structure, Herrnstein Smith explains that such dualisms:

> Require us to posit the existence of two independent levels of narrative structure: the first or basement level, underlying every narrative, is its "deep structure" or "basic story;" The second or upper level is the narrative discourse itself, where the basic story is "actualized," "realized," "expressed," or "manifested" in some form—or in many different forms, modes, media, and thus, versions (Herrnstein Smith, 1981, p. 210)

Research on personal narratives suggests that an analysis of the recit, offers an important way of understanding the importance of storytelling process on the tellers.

Herrnstein Smith (1981) explains that narrators construct their "versions" or recit based on the motives and interests such selections can serve:

> For any given narrative, there is always multiple basic stories that can be constructed in response to it because basic-ness is always arrived at by the exercise of some set of operations, in accord with some set of principles, that reflect some set of interests, all of which are, by nature, variable and thus multiple. . . . The form and features of any "version" of a narrative will be a function of, among other things, the particular motives that elicited it and the particular interests and functions it was designed to serve (p. 217)

Similarly, Kerby (1991) suggests that narrative is "unavoidably selective." Lucaites and Condit (1983) explain that "in rhetorical discourse, the narrator must select and integrate only those elements of a story that make it persuasive to a specific audience" (p. 95). Further, Langellier (1989) maintains:

> In narratives of personal experience, the narrative event emphasizes the personal as it features a first-person narrator . . . relating an experience from his or her perspective. The narrated event highlights the experience because the event it retells is from the teller's own life. The effect of telling a personal narrative is to enhance experience as expressivity exceeds referentiality to create a possible world (p. 255)

Abuse survivors construct their narrative "versions" to facilitate narrative sensemaking and teller empowerment. As I examined the narratives collected for this study, I found that the survivors use the narrative event to "create a possible world," by positioning themselves in varying degrees of empowered statuses during their recountings.

The narrators' recit, which is manifested in their use and re-use of certain thematic references, or survivor discourse, seems to be directly related to the levels of independence from the abuser they currently enjoy. "Survivor discourse" refers to thematic references used by abuse survivors in their narrative recountings of their experiences. In the narratives for this study, narrators used the recit to position themselves as survivors pursuing independence, survivors maintaining independence, and as survivors living independently.

Survivors who are pursuing independence include those individuals who were only recently separated from their abusers, such as clients of Haven House. These survivors all stressed their responsibility to their dependents as their primary reason for leaving their abusive mates, as well as their source of strength for staying away. One narrator explained, "this is not what I wanted for my kids, so we pulled out." When I asked this narrator how she survived day by day, she replied:

> Kids. It's the only reason I get up. It's the only reason I lay down at night. I thank God for another, every day. And, I've learned the hard way to take it one day at a time. One day . . . I'm trying to teach my kids respect, honor. A woman is to be respected, any woman, period, is to be respected.

Similarly, another narrator explained her reason for seeking shelter at Haven House, she asked herself:

> What do I have to do to make it easier on my little girl? I don't want—I mean, it's a shame for a child to have to look at her father and say, "Daddy, why are

you doing these things to her?" Or, for him to look at her and call her a little bitch, and she's just a baby. So, I ended up here, and here I am starting all over again. And for a while, I cried and was lost. I just kind of held on to my baby and said, "well, this is all I've got, so I've got to take it from here."

In this excerpt, the narrator stresses that responsibility to her daughter provoked her to seek help, as she asked herself what she must do "to make life easier for my daughter?" Further, her daughter's well being gives her the strength to stay away, because she claims, "this is all I've got."

Each of the survivors I interviewed at Haven House are parents. Throughout their narratives, the survivors spent a significant amount of time referencing their children. Even when the narrators disclosed other details of their lives, they almost always returned to discourse regarding their children. Consequently, those who have recently separated from their abusive mates, used survivor discourse which focused on their ability to separate from their abusers based on the needs of others. Through the recit, they positioned themselves as survivors who are pursuing independence, rather than those who have realized full independence from their abusers. This seems to indicate that these survivors are placing themselves in a lower—empowered position, perhaps, than a survivor who emphasizes alternative roles for themselves or a reconceptualization of experience, where they emphasize a shift away from victim blame. Such more-empowered positions would indicate a survivor who is maintaining independence from the abuser, rather than pursuing it.

For other survivors, the recit also reflected levels of independence from their abusers. Those who believe that their abusers continue to pose a real threat to them used survivor discourse which positioned them as individuals who are trying to maintain independence from their abusers. For example, these narrators referenced the perceived threat of injury or loss or the perceived power hierarchies that existed in their lives. Although one narrator has been separated from her abuser for years, she continues to fear for her life and her child's well being. Consequently, when narrating her experience, the survivor discourse she used and re-used frequently touched on the fear she still feels. At the close of the interview, for example, she re-emphasized her sense of fear:

I believe he doesn't know where I am, because he hasn't tried to find me. Because he's maybe, I guess, I believe that . . . I don't know what would happen if he were to contact me again, I—I do think I could handle it a little bit better, but maybe not. You know, I still look behind me. I still know who's behind me. I still know who's around me—all of the time.

This woman's reuse of survivor discourse regarding the fear she felt represents how she positions herself as a survivor. While telling her story, she described the great strides and accomplishments she has made in achieving her personal goals, yet she also described how she is haunted by the possibility of future interaction with her abuser. Significantly, she closed the interview session by re-emphasizing her present sense of fear. Despite the independence she has gained from leaving her abuser, she emphasized fear throughout her narration. Additionally, she pointed to her position in her "future story" as someone who must work to maintain independence, while continually living in fear.

Another narrator explained that although she was awarded full custody of her children after her divorce, she still confronts the threat of losing her children:

> I was fortunate to have a judge that was able to see through him. And, being awarded custody of the kids when they're with him, for the weekend, or when they are away with him on vacation. It's always in the back of my mind that they may not come back. And, it's like a living hell.

This narrator is an empowered survivor who must maintain independence. Although she is independent of her abuser's control, in that, she is divorced and is the custodial parent of her children, she is neither fully independent nor fully empowered. The potential behavior of her abuser can control the degree of her emotional independence, in that, she cannot be free of him when her children are in his care. Consequently, the ambiguous nature of independence which is in flux, keeps her from asserting empowered survivor discourse, which is reflected in the recit of survivors who are clearly independent from their abusers.

Those narrators who position themselves as survivors living independently, disclosed little fear of interacting with their abusers in the future. These narrators include individuals who have been separated from their abusers for long periods of time, by geographical location, and so forth. These narrators selected survivor discourse which included frequent references to personal achievement, confronting uncertainty, reconceptualization of experience, and emphasis of alternative roles. For example, of those narrators who are positioned as independent from their abusers' control, sixty-six percent discussed the need to educate others about abuse or their desire to become actively involved in facilitating change in a victim's life. One survivor stated:

> If I had to go back and do it again, I can't really say I'd do it differently, because, I wouldn't be where I am now. So, I'm hopefully going to be working at the Women's Center here in [   ]. It's something I've always wanted to do. And because I don't direct my energy towards my relationship with Bob, right now, I feel like I want to use that time to put in, to help women who have just

come out of or are in situations of domestic violence. Hopefully, my experience, my true hope, as opposed to my false hope that I used to have, can help somebody else.

In this quote, the narrator demonstrates her empowered position by emphasizing her personal achievement of overcoming her involvement with an abusive mate, as well as her alternative role as a potential role model for present victims of domestic violence. I found this to be the case throughout her interview transcript in which she references her empowered status several times.

References to the need to get involved, to educate and assist others, and so forth, represent survivor discourse used by those survivors who are free from future interaction from their abusers. Additionally, such references were highlighted in the discourse of the staff narratives as well. Each of the staff members interviewed for this study, alluded to the importance of taking control away from the abuser and moving the site of personal control to the victim. This strategy was reflected in the narrators' positioning of themselves according to the survivor discourse they included in their storytelling. The more control they assumed over their life decisions and actions, the more empowered they positioned themselves in their survivor discourse and the recit.

The survivors' recit is influenced by the socio-economic class the survivor belongs to as well. For example, those narrators who belong to a lower socio-economic class made many more references to the financial constraints they faced when separating themselves from their abusers. One narrator, who belongs to a lower socio-economic class, made twelve references to financial problems she confronted when leaving her abusive mate. Issues of economic insecurity recurred significantly less often in the survivor discourse of the narrators who belong to middle or upper socio-economic classes, except in references to a reduction of their previous financial standing, which resulted from their decision to leave. For example, such a referencing occurred in one middle-class narrative only twice in the interview session. Consequently, the selection of survivor discourse is often the result of situational and social contexts which surround the telling of the narrative, as well as the daily issues of survival that each of the narrators confront. The following excerpt will serve as an example of how the recit, which includes specific survivor discourse, can enhance narrative sensemaking for the narrator and the listener. In this excerpt, the speaker explains how her feelings of lack of recourse against her abuser's dominance led to self-destructive behavior on her part:

And then all of a sudden, I get up one morning, and he's gone. And, I'm like, this isn't right. Now see what he did was, he just worked it in perfectly so he had joint custody too, so I couldn't say anything about him leaving. So, when he left, he had contacted his attorney, and told his attorney that I was, I wasn't stable, and that they thought I was headed for a nervous breakdown and some other things, and he got a signed statement from the doctor that said he thought I was headed for a nervous breakdown. So, then the court gave him full custody of my kids. So, I battled with that for a long time. After I lost my kids, then, I had just given up, and I went to drinking and doing drugs and everything, which landed me in prison. I went to prison for three years and seven months. And, the whole time I was in prison, I was thinking about, God, I have never really done anything to hurt anybody, why am I suffering so much? Why is my life such a living hell? I'm a good mother, I was a good wife. I worked hard. I never stole from anybody. I don't lie to anybody. What's wrong? You know? And, my situation was going pretty much, I was at the wrong place at the wrong time. You know, it wasn't that I was really doing anything wrong, I just got mixed up with the wrong people, and everybody ended up going to jail.

In her recit, this narrator chooses specific survivor discourse to include, to project her version of her life experiences. For example, she includes a discussion of why she believes she engaged in "drinking and doing drugs and everything," that it resulted from her abuser's control over their children, and the lack of recourse she experienced when confronting her abuser, the doctor, and judicial system, which removed the children from her custody. Her line of reasoning, that her negative behavior which "landed" her in prison, was a result of circumstances beyond her control, places her in the position of a disempowered victim. This discourse choice emphasizes her contention that "I'm a good mother. I was a good wife," and "it wasn't that I was really doing anything wrong." Inclusion of such rationalization in her narrative discourse allows her to conceptualize or give meaning to her experience in a manner which seems to lesson her sense of culpability or responsibility. This is consistent with Richardson's (1990) notion that narrative is "a distinctive way of ordering experience and constructing reality" (p. 118), as well as Richardson's (1990) contention that "telling one's story gives meaning to the past from the point of view of the present and future" (p. 126). Consequently, she is constructing a reality for herself and her listener, which reflects her past feelings of victimization and lack of control over her own life. This places her in a more positive position, a position for which she sets down the criteria. For example, she explains why she is "good," when she explains " I worked hard. I never stole from anybody. I don't lie to anybody," and so forth.

Choices surrounding what survivor discourse to include also involves excluding material from the narrative recounting. Although it would be impossible to know all of the choices of survivor discourse which were excluded from her recit, she may have chosen to omit details about the nature of the doctor's letter, the judge's decision, how her husband obtained joint custody to begin with, and so forth. This narrator's story serves as an example of how narrators can use storytelling to facilitate their own narrative sensemaking. Whether consciously or unconsciously, the narrator's recit and use of survivor discourse frames the audiences' responses to the narrated events. In her narrative performance, this narrator is able to project a positive or empowered position for herself as a person who has overcome the adversity of domestic violence and abuse. Further, she positions herself a s a person who is taking positive steps for her and her daughter's future, as she continues in the interview session. Her recit, and selection of survivor discourse, ultimately influences the listener's reaction to her narrative performance. As the narrator receives a positive or empathic response from her listener (which she did in the interview session in which she told me this story), she is able to audience my audiencing, which further aides narrative sensemaking on her part. For example, if she can narrate this story to someone else and receive a positive response, she is, perhaps, further validating the original perspective she sought to share through her narrative performance originally. Consequently, the listener is aided in narrative sensemaking by the use of survivor discourse. Such discourse contributed to the framing and explaining of the previous life experiences of the narrator, which is perceived by the listener, in the listener's attempt to gain understanding and increase narrative sensemaking. Selection of alternative details of discourse, such as details describing the specific actions which led to her arrest, could have resulted in an alternative perception of the narrated event by both the narrator and/or the listener, that is, it might have resulted in alternative narrative sensemaking by the participants. The degree to which the narrators see themselves as empowered, or imagine future empowered statuses is indicated in how they position themselves, that is, what empowered status they assume in their narrative recounting. Their recit, as well as the specific survivor discourse they used in their storytelling, aided the survivors' narrative sensemaking for the listeners, as well as themselves, by scrutinizing and justifying the decisions and actions they took to facilitate change in their lives.

USE OF THEMES

As I examined the narratives collected for this study, I found that the survivors often used combinations of themes as they presented their "versions" of their life experiences. In the following pages, I will describe how the narrators used combinations of themes to facilitate narrative sensemaking.

Themes of disempowerment were often used together, for example, themes of traditional roles often led to a discussion of perceived power dynamics (in 83% of the interview sessions), or a discussion of relational loyalty (in 42% of the interview sessions). In the following excerpt, one woman recounts her experience giving birth to a male child, using paired themes of disempowerment:

> I was very excited. I think that I had stepped back from the relationship because I was nested and preparing for this child . . . there was this big thing about having a boy. This child needs to be a boy. Oh, my God, I was so guilty when [   ] was born, and it was a girl, it was such a horrible feeling. You know, on the one hand, not to have pleased him, and on the other hand, not to love my daughter, or feel that right away, you know, instead, that disappointment that this was not a boy. And [   ] was really pissed that this was not a boy, and that was really hard.

Issues of traditional roles are evidenced in conflicting utterances drawn from this excerpt. For example, this survivor explains that she "nested" and "prepared" for her child, that she "needed" to have a boy in order to "please" her husband. This viewpoint reflects a very traditionally oriented view of the role of mother as nurturer, as well as the need for a wife to please her husband with a male offspring. Such views are embedded in traditional roles and patriarchy. As she continues this story, she explains that it was "a horrible feeling," that "was really hard" for her. With these remarks, she is commenting upon her prior conformity to traditional roles as quite negative, inferring that complacency regarding traditional roles characterized her abusive relationship.

Perceived power, which often involves male dominance over women, explains this narrator's desire to "please" her husband through the birth of an "appropriate" offspring. This is evidenced as she recounts, "this child needs to be a boy . . . I was so guilty when [   ] was born, and it was a girl, it was such a horrible feeling." Additionally, her spouse's anger, that she describes when she says "[   ] was really pissed that this was not a boy," coupled with her sense of "disappointment that this was not a boy," emphasizes the issue of power dynamics and the hierarchical relationship that existed between her and her abusive mate. Another example of paired themes of disempowerment occurs in the following excerpt:

> Another thing that has to do with domestic violence is not being able to make ends meet. You know, you strive and you strive and you keep trying to do better and the government is steadily slapping your benefits down or whatever, and like the steel mills getting laid off. A lot of guys got laid off, so when they got laid of, they went home and bitched at their wives and then the bills piled up. And then, all of a sudden, you've got a bunch of fighting and arguing and a bunch of going out and getting drunk and coming home and beating up your kids and your wife. And, it really stinks, cause I can't get a job, and I can't take care of them. I don't feel like a man anymore.

In this quote, the speaker uses two themes of disempowerment, including economic insecurity and traditional roles. Her references to the difficulties survivors face as they confront loss of benefits while "you strive and strive and keep on trying to do better," indicate that achieving independence from an abuser is contingent upon economic security of the survivor.

Her explanation of how a man who is laid off from work will engage in domestic violence, because he doesn't "feel like a man anymore," reinforces traditional stereotypical roles that a man must be the financial provider for the family, and failure to do so reduces his masculinity.

Instances of recurring themes of empowerment used together, for example, reconceptualization of the experience while assessing the costs of the relationship, were used in the survivor narratives as well. In the following excerpt, the narrator uses a combination of three themes of empowerment including personal achievement, rejection of constraints and responsibility to her dependents:

> I have a daughter that's going to be ten in a couple of months, and she is probably the kind of daughter that every feminist would dream of having. She's independent, she's self assured. She's not gonna take any crap off of anybody, especially males. She already has, not a negative, but a cautious orientation toward men and boys who think that they can over power or demean her. She's intelligent. She has a wonderful personality, and she clams she's not getting married ever in her life. I keep telling her, as well as my sons, that they are not, that they're not allowed to get married until they've completed their college education. I'd like for them to be free thinkers, individuals, and to be all that they can possibly be.

As she delivered this quote, the narrator did so with an air of confidence and pride that she had some how provided for this "free thinking," that her daughter's feminist ideals, her belief that her daughter is "independent and self assured" at ten years old, is in part, a personal achievement of her mother's positive influences. She describes how her daughter "won't take crap off of anybody," referring to rejecting the constraints a female may be subjected to in a patriarchal society. Further, she explains her desire to protect her children from entering marriage before they're ready, that they are "not allowed to get married until they completed their college education." She seems to believe that her responsibility to her dependents requires that she encourage them to pursue an education as a means of preparing them for future independence. This narrator's use of thematic combinations of empowerment reflect the importance of narrator positioning in the construction of the future story. By engaging in positive survivor discourse, this narrator is strategically setting the stage for her continued empowerment. She envisions herself as a positive and necessary influence on her children. In that sense, she is using the narrative event as a means of constructing a life without her abuser, as a means of reinforcing her own independence and strength.

Perhaps most significant is when the thematic combinations borrow from themes of disempowerment and themes of empowerment consecutively. This is significant in that it can represent a struggle in the narrative sensemaking by the tellers, who are uncertain about how they are positioning themselves during these moments of storytelling. One example of such a combination occurred frequently in the narratives collected for this study. In seventy-five percent of the narratives, discourse regarding traditional roles was located or positioned next to discourse regarding responsibility to dependents. The following excerpt reflects this type of combination:

> My son was getting as tall as he was, or taller, he's like six-two, and in the meantime, I had like four girls in a row. And, in a sense, I often wondered if it was just a blessing there was only one of the kind like him, so to speak, cause if I had to have three girls, you know what I'm saying, four boys, oh God, will they be like this to their girlfriends or wives . . . you think about stuff like that . . . protect your girls from their boyfriend or husband.

This woman's claim that she "wondered if it was just a blessing there was only one of the kind like him," reflects an acceptance of traditional roles, that is, a stereotype that a child will act in similar ways as the same sex parent, for example, the boys becoming abusers or the girls becoming victims. At the same time, she references her traditional role as a mother who needs to protect her children, that one must "protect your girls from their boyfriend or husband."

Through her assertion, "you think about stuff like that . . . protect your girls," this excerpt is framed by the narrator's sense of responsibility to her dependents, that she must protect them, by removing them from the abuse. This sense of responsibility places her in a more empowered position than does acceptance and/or conformity to traditional roles.

Positioning oneself in the survivor discourse is an important way in which the survivors can begin to envision themselves as empowered individuals. How survivors present and perceive the survivor discourse can impact the degree of empowerment that is realized. For example, responsibility to dependents can be perceived as disempowering or empowering by the narrator. When traditionally considered a part of a "woman's role" to care and nurture for her dependents, responsibility to dependents could be disempowering by confining a woman to "her place." However, responsibility to dependents can be empowering, in that, proactive individuals who recognize their responsibility to protect or care for their dependents will often act in ways which are not consistent with traditional roles. For example, a traditionally-oriented woman might believe that she should not work outside of the home or that she must be dependent upon her spouse. Instead, a person responsible to dependents might find outside employment or confront male/abuser dominance in an effort to provide for the dependents, in addition to assuming the traditional role of "nurturer." Finally, this narrator's projection that one must "protect your girls from their boyfriend or husband" further emphasizes her sense of responsibility to her dependents, and the possibility that she may have to actively protect them in the future.

In the following example, the speaker uses a disempowered-empowered combination. In this excerpt, references to perceived power dynamics facilitates a discussion of alternative roles:

> I heard the screaming in the basement once again. My mom was down there, she was trying to console him. She was like so petrified of what he was going to do, or how he was going to act about it. And I heard him scream at her . . . and dicing her to pieces, and my mom was a fragile person sometimes. She's hardened up through the years, cause of him, she's really hardened up. She was crying and that, and she just gave up and went upstairs, and I heard her crying in the living room. I can't stand hearing my mom cry, just being her son. Now, I'm taking this protective type attitude and I came down and told her I was sorry, and she said she was sorry and she can't talk to him. He get so angry. And we sat there and held each other for a while, and I was so furious at my father for doing that to her.

In this passage, the narrator beings explaining the power dynamics which occurred in the hierarchy of his family structure. He alludes to his father's ability to reduce his mother's self esteem, by "dicing her to pieces," however, he also speaks of his emergence as his mother's "protector." While this could be understood as yet another example of perceived power or traditional roles in that his mother is a female who could be "protected" by her male son; the narrator describes his behavior differently than he labels it. He explains that he comforted and held his mother. This behavior highlights alternative roles that he assumed during this time, possibly the role of protector, but more likely, the role of comforter or friend or ally against their mutual abuser. In any case, original feelings of disempowerment which were disclosed in references to power dynamics, yielded the expression of empowered roles of protector, comforter, survivor. In the context of the entire interview session, this act of comforting becomes a significant step in this victim's transcendence to survivorship. Rather than remaining in his room, isolated from the conflict between his parents, he chose risk, to take assertive action to relieve his mother's emotional pain.

Abuse survivors interviewed for this study, used combinations of themes of disempowerment, empowerment, and disempowerment-empowerment themes to facilitate narrative sensemaking for themselves and their listeners. Combinations of themes, like the narrator's recit and survivor discourse assisted the narrators in assuming empowered positions within their storytelling. For example, narrators' references to past states of disempowerment regarding issues of traditional roles, power, lack of recourse and so forth, often led to discussions of the empowered statuses they currently assume.

Thematic combinations facilitated sensemaking and guided discussions regarding transcendence by demonstrating how the narrators move from victimization to survivorship in subtle, and sometimes very explicit ways. The narrators explained their negative experiences, and through the narrative act, were able to reflect and comment upon how they emerged from disempowerment.

THE NATURE OF THE DISCOURSE

The nature of the discourse contained in abuse survivor narratives assists the survivors in narrative sensemaking as well. After conducting a close reading of the narratives, I found that abuse survivors often use dramatic references in their storytelling, as well as meta-critiques, to aid in sensemaking for themselves and their listeners. In the following pages, I will examine how the nature of the discourse enhances sensemaking.

Emphasis of Dramatic References

Emphasizing dramatic references in their storytelling assists narrative sensemaking. By dramatic references, I am referring to the use of emotionally graphic, sensational and/or shocking language and descriptions of narrated events. The following quote reflects one woman's use of dramatic references:

> The first time he ever beat me, he took a vacuum cleaner hose and he beat me so bad, he busted six of my ribs on this end, he broke my nose, he split it wide open. You can see the scar. And he split both of my eyes open. He hit me right across here with that. And I looked like, if you have ever seen that movie, "The Elephant Child," that's how I looked, my whole head was swollen. I looked like a monster.

By emphasizing dramatic references, the narrator is emphasizing the severity of her situation. Her discussion then leads to a description of her feelings of lack of recourse, that without any social network, she was compelled to stay with her abuser. Similarly, another narrator recounts the effects of her abuse, which involved lowering her self esteem, and engaging in drug taking:

> At one point in time, I was digging holes in my face. I would, I had done some LSD 25, and I was tripping my ass off, and I looked in the mirror and I had all these little holes that I had dug in my face, just from my nerves. I mean, I'm talking serious holes. Something inside me clicked.

Once again, this narrator is highlighting the dramatic through her graphic emphasis and re-emphasis on the physical pain she was inflicting upon herself. As I listened to the narratives, each narrator selected specific dramatic references to highlight as a means of convincing me of the seriousness or significance of their abuse. Bennet (1986) explains that, "the story, like the abstract description it is embedded in, is task related. It is designed to explicate a complex viewpoint by embodying it in a simple personal example" (p. 4). Emphasizing the dramatic seems to serve narrative sensemaking in that, the narrators are reinforcing their decision to leave the relationship by focusing on the significant, dangerous incidents they endured. Additionally, the narrators aid the listeners' sensemaking through the use of the dramatic references which reinforce or explain not only their decision to leave, but their claim to membership as a past victim and a current survivor, as well. While non-dramatic references may aid in narrative sensemaking as well, it seems significant that all of the narrators highlighted the dramatic as they recounted their stories of abuse. By emphasizing the dramatic incidents, they emphasized the degree to which they were victimized in their relationships. In a sense, they seemed to be trying to make a case for their claim to victim and/or survivor membership. Further, they emphasized the significance of their transcendence to survivorship as they demonstrated the serious life dramas they confronted and eventually overcame.

The Meta-Critique

One significant strategy that emerged in the narratives collected for this study includes the narrators' use of their storytelling as a critique or commentary on their experiences, and their past perceptions of these experiences. These meta-critical analyses are manifested through the narrators' accounts of their past and current perceptions of their states of mind and of their life conditions, as they continue to move from roles of victim to survivor. Their analyses, which are facilitated by the narrative event, function in two significant ways. First, as a means for the narrators to recognize or conceptualize their experience. Second, as a tool available to help the tellers to assess the triumph over the adversity in their lives. The following discussion will focus on how the survivors used their own meta-critique to facilitate transcendence from victimization to survivorship.

The use of narrative recounting, using a meta-critical stance, assists survivors in confronting significant issues regarding their abuse. As I examined the narratives collected for this research, by conducting an analysis of the rhetorical strategies embedded in the narrative recit, I found that the meta-critique became an important means of transcendence for the survivors. As they recounted their stories, the survivors identified three issues regarding their abuse, that they needed to overcome to bring change to their lives. Through their meta-critiques, the narrators confronted (1) a previous failure to act against abuse, (2) engaging in negative coping strategies and, (3) a prior tendency to attribute blame for the abuse to themselves. An analysis of the rhetoric contained in their narrative recountings suggests that these were issues the narrators needed to overcome, in order to define themselves as survivors.

Failure to Act

This issue confronts the victim's failure to remove him or herself from an abusive relationship. Through their narrative recountings and reconceptualization of their experiences, the narrators for this study were able to understand their delay. In the interview sessions, seventy-eight percent of the survivors spent considerable time addressing the issue of failing to act sooner to alleviate the abuse. Sixty-seven percent of the survivors indicated that prior to leaving their abusive mates, they held on to a belief that the abuser would change, and eighty-nine percent believed that their role in the relationship necessitated complacency. These beliefs were cited as primary reasons for remaining in abusive relationships for extended periods of time. All of the survivors volunteered their reasons for remaining, despite the fact that they were not asked to describe this behavior during the interview sessions. In the following excerpt, one woman explains why she remained in an abusive relationship:

> I did fall in love with him, and I cared for him very much. But, looking back, I think it was an unhealthy type of love, I felt like I had to have him, not necessarily that my life was meaningless without him, but that I had greater significance when I was with him—not because of (his profession) because of things that made my life seem complete by being with him. I thought it was a positive thing.

By understanding or reconceptualizing her need to have her abuser in her life, this speaker is better able to assess how she defines her identity without her abuser, how she can position herself independently.

Another example of justifying a failure to act or leave an abusive relationship is explored through references to the abuser's behavior. In this quote, the survivor describes how she was finally able to see through her abuser's behavior:

> I don't know. I just don't know why I stayed with him. It's just something I can't—if he wasn't there, I missed him. But, when he beat me up, I hated him. You know, there were two sides to my husband, that alcoholic side and the drugs and there was him being sober. And, I guess that was what I was holding on to.

Justifying one's failure to leave an abusive relationship, understanding it, and critiquing it, become important steps in the process of transcendence for abuse victims. It serves as a primary means in which the victims "forgive" themselves and begin to position themselves in a more positive way. The narrators for this study used such a personal analysis to facilitate narrative sensemaking for the teller as well as their audience.

Negative Coping Strategies.

Seventy-eight percent of the survivors moved beyond personal justification for staying to explore the negative coping strategies they invoked during the abusive period in their lives. For some, the negative strategies were as subtle as ignoring the abuse or minimizing the seriousness of the abuse. For others, negative coping strategies included self destructive behaviors such as drug or alcohol abuse, eating disorders, attempting or contemplating suicide, engaging in illegal activities such as prostitution, and so forth. In the following excerpt, a survivor explains how she used food for comfort, rather than confronting issues of the abuse she experienced:

> I've always—for most of my life, I've been overweight. At some point, a couple of times, I was well over 200 pounds. I wouldn't confront, I would eat, I would eat. It would keep me quiet. And the nurturing soft mushy food really, and when you're mad, you eat crunchy food. It's very obvious once you step back and take a look at it, but of course, I never bothered to do that.

This narrator was eventually able to identify the negative coping behavior that she invoked. By reflecting and commenting upon her eating "disorder," the narrator came to understand how eating was a comfort to her, a way for her to suppress her need to confront issues of abuse that troubled her. This type of self critique is an important way for the survivor to alter future behavior which could be potentially damaging to her. Other narrators described their reliance on alcohol or drugs to comfort them in periods of abuse. Determining the root of such self destructive behavior can enable a survivor to overcome such behavioral patterns, and further, place him or herself in a higher empowered status. Similarly, the following description demonstrates how one victim coped with abuse by immersing herself in alternative activities. She excelled in work and school in an effort to ignore the impact her childhood abuse was having on her life as an adult:

> At work, I was the epitome of efficiency. I, everybody loved me. I was jovial, funny, bright, and smart, and articulate and organized, and great ideas, and I was throwing all my energy into school and work, and it was an obsession so I wouldn't have to deal with—I was 4.0 at school, incredible at work, but the inside of me was falling apart fast.

Despite the positive gains she achieved academically and professionally, this behavior was perpetuating the silence in her life. Such silence about abuse, restricts a victim from confronting abuse, and consequently, transcendence to survivorship is stifled.

Hence, by examining the negative coping strategies and critiquing these past behaviors, the narrators can reflect upon the levels of progress they have made in overcoming the issues invoked by their abuse, issues which had previously stifled their transcendence to survivors.

Victim Blame

Many narrators described their past feelings of culpability and/or complacency regarding their abuse. Victim blame was noted by eighty-nine percent of the survivors. Through their self-critiques, the narrators are better able to understand their past feelings regarding their role in the abuse, and come to recognize that the true source of abuse, was the abuser's behavior:

> I know that I blocked out a lot of memories. He was verbally aggressive. Through—not, not in the first six months of the relationship, but it started the senior year . . . he started to be a bit more verbally aggressive, but this was also at the time when he told me for the first time that he loved me. And, there was one instance where he slapped me on my leg, and it hurt me. And he convinced me that it wasn't meant to be like that, saying my perception was wrong. I shouldn't have felt hurt and there was only two of us in that situation, so I just kind of wrote it off.

During the time of her initial abuse, this narrator was invalidated as a victim; she was convinced that her perceptions were wrong. Such beliefs allow for victims of abuse to attribute blame to themselves, rather than focus on the source of the abuse or recognize the existence of the abuse. A self analysis by the survivor facilitates a shifting of the blame away from the victim to the abuser. Once again, the survivor is positioning her or himself in a stronger position, in this case, a survivor who overcame abuse, that was not a result of her behavior, but that of her abuser.

In summary, the survivors' narrative recounting, which involved their own meta-critique regarding their abuse, served as an important method for the tellers to understand better their involvement in abusive relationships. Their explanations were often based on their own need to justify their involvement and understand their lack of control over the abusers' behaviors. Through the telling of their personal stories, the survivors gain a greater sense of "relief" from their past belief of culpability for the abuse. They are able to "forgive" themselves for remaining in the relationship as long as they did, for engaging in negative behavior to cope with the abuse, and they are assisted in shifting the blame for the abuse to the abuser. These are important steps which can facilitate an individual's transcendence from victimization to survivorship. Through the self critique invoked by the narrative event, the narrators were able to recognize the significance of their triumph over the adversity in their lives, to make sense of where they've been and how they have moved to their current position of empowerment.

DISCUSSION

Using specific survivor discourse in the recit, the use and reuse of combinations of themes, and the dramatic and meta-critical nature of the discourse survivors use in their narrative recountings, all represent ways in which survivors facilitate narrative sensemaking.

Abuse survivors use specific survivor discourse in the recit, which emphasizes their experiences through the narrative event. By carefully using survivor discourse, in an effort to highlight the experiences from their own perspective, the narrative event can become a vehicle for the teller's transcendence. The degree to which the tellers position themselves as empowered in the recit can influence the creation of their future plans for survival.

The use of combinations of themes, or thematic clusters, aids in narrative sensemaking as well. "Thematic clusters" refers to the use of two or more combinations of recurrent themes of disempowerment, empowerment, or disempowerment-empowerment themes used concurrently.

Abuse survivors work through narrative recounting, which often highlights dramatic references and their meta-critique regarding their experiences of abuse, facilitating sensemaking. Through their meta-critique, survivors are able to confront issues of the failure to act to alleviate the abuse, engaging in negative coping strategies, and attribution of victim blame.

Each of the sensemaking strategies assist survivors in coming to terms with their abuse, and moving into empowered positions. Through their storytelling, survivors can gain self-esteem, they can gain assistance from a social network including family, friends, and service providers. Through re-performance of their narratives, they can add to their personal empowerment by positioning themselves as independent individuals who determine their own life stories.

In the following section of this chapter, I will discuss the narrative/performative strategies invoked for the telling of abuse survivor narratives, collected for this study.

PERFORMANCE STRATEGIES

Cultures are most fully expressed and made conscious of themselves in their ritual and theatrical performances. . . . A performance is a dialectic of "flow," that is, spontaneous movement in which action and awareness are one, and "reflexivity," in which the central meanings values and goals of a culture are seen "in action," as they shape and explain behavior. A performance is declarative of our shared humanity, yet it utters the uniqueness of particular cultures. We will know one another better by entering one another's performances and learning their grammars and vocabularies (Turner, 1980, p. 1)

While Turner (1980) references ritual and theatrical performances specifically in this quote, significant parallels can be drawn between theatrically framed performances which occur during the re-telling of an abuse survivor narrative. In this section, I apply a theatrical metaphor to the examination of these narratives, in order to highlight the performance dimensions of the tellings. Goffman (1959) explains how we present ourselves in everyday life:

The legitimate performances of everyday life are not "acted" or "put on" in the sense that the performer knows in advance just what he is going to do, and does this solely because of the effect it is likely to have. The expressions it is felt he is giving off will be especially "inaccessible" to him. But as in the case of less legitimate performers, the incapacity of the ordinary individual to formulate in advance the movements of his eyes and body does not mean that he will not express himself through these devices in a way that is dramatized and pre-formed in his repertoire of actions. In short, we all act better than we know (p. 73–74)

The performance of abuse survivor narratives collected for this study represent incidents in which natural performances of storytelling rely on specific performance strategies, used to enhance the narrative event. Abuse survivors represent an important subculture of individuals who share experiences of victimization, struggle, and empowerment. The life world of abuse survivors is intricately connected to all members of the dominant culture who are subjected to imposed definitions of patriarchal roles and limitations on behavioral expectations according to biological sex, race and class. Performing a survivor narrative becomes a significant means by which members of this subculture achieve identity, and explore possibilities of the empowered status of long-time survivor. Audiencing the performance of survivor narratives can enable a listener to come to know the tellers significantly better.

When telling abuse survivor narratives, storytellers invoke and capitalize on specific performance strategies in an effort to gain a desired response from their listeners. Among these strategies which mirror the strategies of theatrically framed performances are efforts to create characterization, a convincing story line, and setting the stage for transcendence. Robinson (1981) suggests that "a proper accounting of everyday storytelling must take into consideration what story is being told, to whom, when, and for what purposes" (p. 59). Further, Bauman (1986) notes that "the structure of performance events is a product of the systematic interplay of numerous situational factors" (p. 3–4). In the discussion that follows, three primary performance strategies invoked by the narrators for this study (characterization, story line, setting the stage) are scrutinized for significance in promoting listener understanding and teller empowerment.

CHARACTERIZATION: POSITIONING THE PLAYERS

Character is that which revels choice, shows what sort of thing a man (or woman) chooses or avoids in circumstances where the choice is not obvious, so those speeches convey no character in which there is nothing whatever which the speaker chooses or avoids (Aristotle, p. 29)

The telling of an abuse survivor narrative involves many choices. The narrator chooses whether or not to engage in narration, selects details to include or omit, and so forth. Perhaps one of the most significant choices a narrator makes, involves determining how the characters are positioned in the story. This is not to say that this choice is necessarily a conscious decision, but at minimum, this choice which reflects the narrator's self concept and perception of past experiences of abuse. Similar to Loseke's (1992) assertion that a battered woman must conform to a socially constructed "ideal type" of battered woman to be afforded the label of victim, so too must a survivor meet certain criteria to be afforded survivor status. This criteria is determined not only by socially constructed images, but more importantly, in the self evaluation of the survivor of such abuse. In the narratives collected for this study,

I found clearly marked positions or character types for the survivors, their abusers, and their audience. The survivors were often positioned as protagonists, the abusers as antagonists, the audience as agents of empathy. In the section which follows, I will discuss the ways in which the narrators position themselves, their abusers and the audiences of their telling.

Positioning the Narrator

Smiley (1971) defines the role of the protagonist:
   The term protagonist implies involvement in an extended struggle and passion of some sort. To the ancient Greek playwrights, protagonist probably meant first or chief actor; for most modern dramatists, it means the character receiving the most attention from the playwright, the other characters and eventually the audience. The protagonist is the character with the most volition, the one who makes events happen and propels the action. The protagonist's problem, more than that of any character, is centripetal to the plays entire organization. A protagonist is also a key element of the story . . . the chief agent for the reestablishment of balance (p. 96)

In this quote, the author is obviously discussing the structure of playwriting, yet, similar principles were applied by the narrators who constructed their stories of abuse. By positioning themselves as the central characters who propel action and re-establish balance, the narrators assume empowered roles as survivors. Agreeing to be a part of a study about survivors of abuse itself infers that the narrators have labeled themselves as such (as survivors). In their talk, the narrators positioned themselves as protagonists in a variety of ways. For example, the narrators describe themselves as survivors, focus on positive personal achievements, as well as positive future plans. Additionally, some narrators described the assertive role they now assume in caring for themselves and their children. In the following excerpt, a survivor explains her hopes for her children, that they can benefit from what she has learned:

   I want them to know that they have alternatives, that they are free to do whatever they can. They have the intelligence and money is available from somewhere, to help them to do what they can do. For them to self actualize, that is one of my goals in raising these kids, that they can self actualize some time in their lives.

In this quote, the narrator implies that she has been involved in a "struggle" which did not allow her to be "free to do whatever she could." Additionally, by stating that "I want to know," (meaning her children), she is assuming a proactive role, she becomes the character who "makes events happen and propels action," through living and narrating the continuing story of her and her children's lives. By achieving her personal goal of facilitating her children's "self actualization," for example, she does indeed become "the chief agent for the reestablishment of balance," as described by Smiley (1971) in his definition of protagonist. In conducting this interview, I felt that the narrator was speaking not only of her children's future, but her own. This quote demonstrates a positive outlook for the future that she achieved by overcoming her victimization. Later in the same interview, the narrator described an incident of abuse when her husband pulled her around by her hair. She discusses how she dealt with this abuse:

> The next day, I went to a beauty salon and had my hair cut up high on my neck. And when he came home that evening, I was sitting in a chair waiting for him. And when he looked at me, he was shocked because he had always liked long hair and I told him that he would never do that to me again. And that no matter what he did to me, he could keep me from my family, he could beat me, anything that he could possible do to me, anything he could think of—he could do to me—but that he would never break my spirit, that I would not be broken by his abusive devices.

Although the survivor did not leave her abuser at the time of this abusive incident, her behavior marks a performance of empowerment. Her performance of this story within the interview session, displayed pride on her part, her demeanor demonstrated confidence. The choices she made in recounting this story, beginning with a description of the abuse and leading to her act of survival/empowerment, clearly positioned her in the story as the protagonist who moved to facilitate balance in her life, in this case, control over her own body, by cutting her hair and reclaiming a positive self image.

Positioning the Abuser

The narrators frequently positioned the abuser as the antagonist in their stories. Smiley (1971) explains:

> Although a play can well exist without one, an antagonist lends clarity and power to dramatic structure. The primary function of an antagonist is opposition to the protagonist. An antagonist usually best represents the obstacles. If his volition is approximately the same or greater than that of the protagonist, the resultant crises and conflicts will be more dynamic and can more easily reach an optimum level for the specific material. An antagonist frequently is responsible for initiating the protagonists, and the plays crucial problem (p. 97)

In the most of the narratives, the survivors took a significant amount of time recounting details about the abuser's behavior, that clearly positioned the abuser as the antagonist of their story. While this is not at all surprising, it is still quite a significant strategy in empowering the teller. By carefully positioning the abuser as the antagonist, the teller becomes convincingly more so a protagonist who facilitated change, reducing victim blame. Many narrators discussed the imposed interactions they endured with their abuser. In the passage that follows, a survivor explains her grandfather's presence in her life, a situation over which she had no control as a child:

> Um, as far back as I can remember . . . I was abused on a weekly basis by my dad's father. Um, of course, I didn't know what it was or anything. Um, they came over, he was very close with his family . . . this was the patriarch—and my father's name sake, and all that. And, um, they came over every single Sunday. And, if it wasn't a Sunday, it was a Thursday, my father's day off. But, they were there, every single week. And, um, what he would do, which—I didn't get it, was he would hug me and—th—, hug me—turn me around so my back was to him. And he'd have to pick me up, to rub my butt against his groin, so—he was average height, so I had to be little. I remember my feet leaving the floor, and just thinking it was kind of weird—there was like a stick in there. You know, and this just went on. You now, that was it, that was the usual hug.

By describing her abuser's behavior in detail, this narrator clearly establishes him as her antagonist. She compounds the positioning of herself as a victim, and his role as antagonist, through her delivery which is slow and somewhat disfluent, which seems to indicate, in her narrative performance, the intensity of these memories on her current emotional state.

Later, in the interview session, she describes how she was finally able to confront her abusive memories, and talk openly about her experience:

> I'm like in a completely different world then I was six years ago. The metamorphosis, you know, that took place. I'm more open in talking about my history. . . . I talk about it more. It's not a bit—and being around people who talk about it too. . . . I found a lot of healing in talking about it.

In her narrative, she describes her abuser as a person who took advantage of her innocence, a person repeatedly used and mistreated her in their relationship of granddaughter and grandfather (although she labels him, her father's dad). In addition, she explains how she was finally able to speak openly about her abuse. By highlighting the nature of her abuse and the importance of telling on her healing, she positions herself as a person who overcame betrayal and fear, who emerged as a very strong character in her story.

Similarly, another narrator establishes her abuser as the antagonist in her story, as she describes his behavior after their separation:

> I had police reports piled up two inches thick, they could never catch him. I'd come out of work, he was in my car, and that scared me to death. I'd run back in the restaurant, call the police, he's gone. Nobody knows where he went, this kind of stuff. Putting hole shots in my front lawn, breaking my windows on the car, flattening my tires, emptying my gas tank. If I'd come out of a, say if I went out to a bar, and I came out, he'd be standing there with a baseball bat, and he finally broke in one morning, and he was on PCP. And he did this all with his fist, he blackened both of my eyes. I had bruises from the top of my body to the bottom.

Here, the narrator clearly establishes her abusive mate as the antagonist of her story. Positioning the abuser as the antagonist is a necessary step for victims of abuse to make, in order to shift blame away from themselves, and emerge the protagonists or central players of their life stories.

Positioning the Audience

> The audience is the ultimate necessity which gives the playwright's work its purpose and meaning. The laws by which the dramatist creates his product are determined by the use to which the product is to be put. The purpose of the drama is communication: The audience plays, not a passive, but an active part in the life of the play (Lawson, 1960, p. 262)

In addition to positioning the characters in the story being told, the narrators also position the audience in the performance of their narratives. As mentioned in Chapter One, Duranti and Brenneis (1986) contend that others "ratify" our communication, that the interaction, "is something partly constituted, that is, made real, possible, and meaningful, through its use by particular actors at particular times and places" (p. 240). Similarly, Langellier (1983) contends that the audience is "situated simultaneously and ambiguously 'outside' the text as performer and 'inside' the text as witness" (p. 37). Further, she explains:

> The audience is both physically present as a performer and spiritually transcendent to the performance as a witness. The audience is carried away by the performance while simultaneously retaining the distance of self and other awareness; it plays and knows that it is playing (p. 37)

Consequently, the interview sessions involved an establishment of a relationship between the tellers and myself as the interviewer. Some narrators acknowledged my presence verbally in the interview situation, by referring to details they knew about me. When recounting a hypothetical description of abusive individuals, one narrator said, "they don't want you coming home with a bachelor degree, and Ph.D., and they like that, it's like, 'well look what I did.'" I did not meet this narrator prior to the interview. All she knew about me was the information included on the Informed Consent Form and any details the counseling coordinator may have given her prior to the interview. As she discussed education, particularly when she referred to a Ph.D., she gestured toward me as if to remark, "like what you're doing." I believe this was an attempt to establish a relationship between the teller and listener, a way for her to connect with who I am, as she explained some of the most intimate and problematic details of her life.

Another narrator not only acknowledged the listener in the telling, but explained future behavioral expectations for her audience:

> I found a lot of healing in talking about it. But, when I talk to people, as I get to know people, here, well, like any place, it's—that I say that, that—it's my choice to disclose this to you, and this is a private conversation between us. And, if— my relationship evolves to a point and I want to disclose it instead of you telling, this is my history, and its my place to disclose it, and so feel honored, is basically what I tell this person (I told it to), just so we understand each other.

By claiming ownership to her life story, this narrator not only reinforces the role of her audience as a privileged interactant who should respect her disclosure and her decision to tell, but she also reinforces her position as a protagonist, who determines the outcome of her own life story by telling it in her own way.

Achieving audience empathy represents an important step toward transcendence for an abuse victim. Consequently, a significant amount of energy is devoted to achieving such empathy through the narrative performances. Pelias (1992) explains that empathy can occur when a "genuine dialogue" occurs between the speaker and listener. Further, he explains that an individual must "work through three fundamental steps: recognition, convergence, and adoption" (p. 90). Convergence occurs as the speaker and listener "merge":

> In this step in the empathic process, a listener and speaker come together. They form a union or bond. The speaker becomes a part of the listener's affective world. The listeners take in the speaker on an emotional level. Moving beyond a distanced recognition of the speaker's point of view, the listener merges with the speaker. Based upon the speaker's utterance, listeners tap and pull into play their own feelings. Emotions begin to correspond (p. 93)

Narrators who seek such a merger construct their narratives carefully, to promote their interpretation of events, in the minds of their listeners. Bennet
(1986) explains that, "throughout the telling . . . narrators seek not only to explain an experience, but to guard it from hostile criticism and protect their
version of the truth, steering their audience to share their interpretation and
their philosophy" (p. 432).

The narrators interviewed for this study enhanced audience empathy by
strategically emphasizing discourse content which described the severity of
their abuse, the limited control they had over their lives, as well as the power
the abusers assumed in their relationships. For example, in the following excerpt, one narrator emphasizes the severity of her abuse to increase audience
empathy:

> And even if I was holding my kids, he didn't care. If I was holding my kids, he'd
> still beat me. That made no difference. I found myself grabbing my children in
> hopes that he wouldn't hit me then, until after I found out he would still hit me
> when I was holding the kids. My thing was to get the kids out of the way, now.
> Cause if I got hurt, they're going to really get hurt. If he gets—if they get
> punched. Maybe I can handle the punch, but my children can't. And once, he did
> miss me, and he coalcocked a baby I was watching. The baby ended up with a
> black eye, all the way around his face.

Similarly, another narrator describes the severity of his situation:

> He came and slammed me against the wall, and I was just yelling, shit, and
> threw me down the stairs and I wasn't gonna fight back, cause he's like 280, big
> guy, and I have no power against him.

In this excerpt, the narrator not only describes the severity of the abuse he experienced, but also the lack of control he felt in trying to protect himself. The
control that abusers have over their victims can convince the victims that they
have no recourse, except to remain complacent. In the next excerpt, one narrator explains her sense of loss of identity from remaining in an abusive relationship:

> Well, it took a long time to get where I didn't feel like I had an identity anymore.
> It took a long time before I really just felt like, who am I and where am I going?
> Over the years, there was always little parts of me that would say, man this is
> not right. I could have been doing this and this, and then I would just fall back
> in.

Through her narration, this survivor emphasizes the lack of control that she
believed she had over her life. Throughout the recounting of their experience,

the narrators emphasized their perceptions of their experience, including the severity of the abuse, the limited options they could employ, the significant control of their abusers, and so forth, as important means of establishing audience empathy.

Additionally, the teller-listener interaction was often facilitated by the questioning of the narrators, and the mini-conversations which occurred between myself and the narrators during the interviews. Herrnstein Smith (1981) contends that telling a narrative is influenced by the teller's perception of the listener's motive:

> Any narrator's behavior will be constrained in part by various assumptions he will have made concerning his present or presumed audience's motives for listening to him. Although these assumptions will usually be formed on the basis of the narrator's prior knowledge of that audience, they may also be reformed on the basis of feedback from the listener during the transaction itself (p. 230).

In assessing my motives for audiencing the narrators' storytelling, the narrators seem to rely on information gained from the Informed Consent Form and conversations with the Counseling Coordinator of Haven House. Additionally, the open-ended interview format seemed to facilitate greater trust, in that, the narrators generally guided the telling. Overall, the narrators' positioning of me as an audience member led me to believe that the interview sessions were positive experiences for the tellers.

Positioning the narrator, abuser and the audience become important strategies of characterization, that ultimately place the tellers in an empowered status, not only in the story, but in the storytelling performance as well. The narrators choose how to frame the abusive incidents. When the narrators do so in a way that denotes them as strong survivors, they embody that characterization in the performance of their narrative, as well as the performance of their everyday life experiences.

CONVINCING STORY LINE

Throughout the telling of the narratives, the tellers constructed stories of victimization and survivorship in believable and compelling ways, by highlighting the incidents of abuse and outside constraints which they overcame in order to emerge at their current state of empowerment.

Performative believability is an important objective in narrative recounting. Inclusion in the interview session itself represents one measure of performative believability, in that, participants in the study were cast as abuse survivors. However, performative believability went beyond this casting and was reinforced through the construction of a convincing story line. One survivor references the importance of performative believability, when she explains how she hoped for more physical evidence regarding her abuse, for fear she wouldn't be believed in her talk about abuse:

> I started wishing that he'd hit me harder, that he'd break a leg, that he'd hospitalize me, so that somebody would notice. So that it wouldn't just be, [she's] making it up, [she's] crazy.

While this excerpt does not necessarily reflect the narrator's strategy in constructing a believable story line, significantly, she points to a recognized need to construct a believable image of herself as a former victim. In his work on "narrative and the rhetoric of possibility," Kirkwood (1992) claims that "commentary," such as the commentary reflected in the excerpt of the survivor's narrative, "can serve several purposes in a rhetoric of possibility, both with respect to narrated performance and audience performances. First, it may call attention to a performance which otherwise might be overlooked" (p. 40). When the survivor contends that she felt she needed physical evidence to support her claim of victimization, "so that it wouldn't just be, she's making it up," she is calling attention to the possibility of being perceived as a liar or as "crazy," as a result of her narrated discourse. Hence, this reference in her narrative indicates not only her attempt to guide the "rhetoric of possibility," but the rhetoric of plausibility as well.

Similarly, another survivor explains how she became accustomed to telling lies to her abuser and others regarding her past experiences in life. During the interview, she explained that she was frequently accused of lying by her abuser, until lying eventually became habitual. When she began to openly tell others about the "truth" of her experiences, she was validated. In this excerpt, she describes how she recognized the benefits of being believed:

> I had a lot of people at the Burnham Fellowship Club that were like old timers that had been around the block. They hadn't been where I had been, but they had seen some really hard times, and they took me in. They kept me busy, and everybody believed what I said, instead of telling you you're a liar. Cause it got to the point, no matter whether I told the truth, or whether I was lying, I wasn't believed for a long time. "You could look me straight in the eyes and I wouldn't know if you were lying and you're an asshole." And I said, "Yeah, but I learned from the best asshole I know. (laughs). I'm striving to be perfect like you." That used to really piss [her abuser] off. Yeah, I've been very open . . . my mom has told me time and time again, don't let people know about your past. Don't tell people about your past, because people are ugly and this and that. But, that's not me. I can't live like that.

In this quote, the narrator highlights the importance of being open. By narrating her experience to others, she was able to begin her necessary transition to survivorship.

A desire to be believed is an important need for a victim of abuse to fulfill in order to transcend to a survivor of abuse. If victims cannot convince themselves or others that they are abuse victims, who are not at fault for their abuse, that the abuse truly exists, they will not be able to recast themselves as survivors.

To facilitate performative believability, the narrators constructed stories with believable progressions of action. Lawson (1960) explains one way of constructing dramatic composition:

> If we observe an action as we perform it in our daily experience, we find that any action (regardless of its scope) consists in (a) the decision (which includes the consciousness of the aim and of the possibilities of its accomplishment); (b) the grappling with difficulties (which are more or less expected because the decision has included a consideration of possibilities); (c) the test of strength (the moment toward which we have been heading, having done our best to evade or overcome the difficulties, we face success or failure of the action); (d) the climax (the moment of maximum effort and realization) (p. 245)

This construction is quite similar to the strategies the narrators used to construct stories of abuse. Revisiting the following narrative excerpt will demonstrate the dramatic composition outlined by Lawson (1960):

> I remember one night I didn't want him to go to a party, because it was with the [   ] department and he was the loverboy of the [   ]. And, we got into an argument. He started hitting me, and at that time I had long hair, probably down to the middle of my back, and he took me from one end of the apartment to the other by pulling my hair. He pulled me around the apartment with my hair. And, I was screaming and it happened to be in the fall and we had our, the glass sliding doors open and someone called the police, After that, I just let him go to any parties he wanted to. I didn't press any charges, I didn't make out a police report. I didn't even go to the door to see the policeman, because I was afraid of what might happen. And, at that point I really wasn't ready to leave him and give him up. But, the next day, I went to a beauty salon and had my hair cut up high on my neck. And when he came home that evening, I was sitting in a chair waiting for him. And he was shocked because he always liked long hair. And I told him that he would never do that to me again. And, that no matter what he did to me, he could keep me from my family, he could beat me, anything that he could possibly do to me, anything he could think of—he could do to me— that he would never break my spirit, that I would not be broken by his abusive devices.

In this narrative, the survivor describes her action, which begins with her decision to stand up to her spouse and tell him that she "didn't want him to go to a party." As a result of her decision, she is faced with severe difficulties, which are manifested in her spouse's physical abuse against her, "he took me from one end of the apartment to the other pulling my hair." Her test of strength is demonstrated as she recounts her retaliation against his behavior, that she "went to the beauty salon and had my hair cut up high on my neck . . . he always liked long hair. And I told him that he would never do that to me again." Facing the success or failure of her action, she sits in "a chair waiting for him." The climax is realized as she recounts, "he was shocked." The accomplishment of her action is emphasized as she recounts her comment to him that "he would never break my spirit, that I would not be broken by his abusive devices."

During the interview sessions, the narrators described their struggles with leaving their partners/abusers, confronting the constraints of economic insecurity, responsibility to dependents, feelings of loneliness, how they grappled with these difficulties before leaving their abusers, and so forth. They disclosed how their decisions to leave influenced their lives, and most reported significant progress of transformation toward survivorship and independence as their "maximum effort" paid off in enhancing their individuality, and the point of this realization. Describing the details regarding the stories of their transcendence promoted performance believability to a significant degree.

Offering compelling details in their narrative discourse became another way in which convincing story lines were constructed by the narrators. Lucaites and Condit (1983) contend, "in rhetorical discourse, the narrator must select and integrate only those elements of a story that make it persuasive to a specific audience" (p. 95). Similarly, Herrnstein Smith (1981) suggests that as we cut back certain details of discourse, we do so to meet certain purposes:

> Whenever we start to cut back, peel off, strip away, lay bare, and so forth, we always do so in accord with certain assumptions and purposes which, in turn, create hierarchies of relevance and centrality; and it is in terms of these hierarchies that will distinguish certain elements and relations, as being central or peripheral, more important or less important, more basic or less basic (p. 217).

To advance a convincing story line, then, the narrators used compelling details formed in the disclosure of mini-dramas of abuse and survival. These mini-dramas were placed in higher "relevance and centrality" by the narrators, and highlighted in their discussion. One such example follows:

> He told me that if I pursued this divorce, that he was going to go into the courtroom, during this divorce proceeding, shoot my lawyer, and watch me go crazy. This was his, that was his goal. He wanted to see me go crazy. But then, later

on, he said, "You know—the lawyer, well, you better tell him that his days are numbered, and it's your fault. You will have his blood on your hands.

This excerpt is an example of a mini-drama, or smaller story within the larger context of the narrative gathered in the interview session that I shared with this survivor. As this narrator included the excerpt, she placed it in a higher position within the "hierarchy" of her narration, through her emphasis of dramatic references in her language, which ultimately re-emphasized the potential abuse she still fears.

By selecting compelling mini-dramas surrounding their abuse, the narrators are constructing a convincing story line, which re-emphasizes their strength in overcoming the abuse.

SETTING THE STAGE FOR TRANSCENDENCE

Another performative strategy invoked by the narrators included in this study was their use of discourse in setting the stage for transcendence. The narrators reflected upon the differing stages of transcendence, and perpetuated further transcendence through narrative performance. Stages of transcendence reflected through the narrative discourse include initial expository statements regarding the perceived need to transcend, discussions of struggling for transcendence, and the realization that change occurred in their lives.

Within the expository statements, the narrators established important relationships between the story telling components, that aided in their reflection of transcendence. Sullivan (1986) explains the function of narration in establishing relationships:

> Stories help people cope. The ability to cope draws its effect from the combination of multiple relationships entailed by narrative communication. Telling a story establishes relationships between the following elements: the narrator and the listener, the narrator and the story; the listener and the story; the narrator and the self, the narrator and the associations of experience, the listener and associations of experience (p. 117).

By establishing such relationships, the narrators were able to lay the groundwork for personal reflection through the performance of their narrative discourse. The following excerpt reflects an expository paragraph that established such groundwork:

> he told me if I wouldn't go with him, he would take the kids and he would go. At that time I called the State Department and asked them to do something about

this, and they told me that if I did not leave him, if I did not separate from him, there's nothing they could do, that I had to go to a civil court, and that it was a civil matter, and I had to work it out first through separation and a possible divorce before I prohibit him from taking the kids out of the country . . . so, the State Department was no help. I think the only thing they did offer me was the fact that I had to make something concrete, before I could get help from anyone.

Through these words, the narrator establishes important groundwork for future narration. She is establishing or positioning herself in the story, allowing the listener entrance into the story. This event, for her, marked a time when she realized that she must take positive steps on her own to facilitate change in her life, it marks the beginning of her transcendence. Her narrative performance marks this period as transitory for both the narrator and the listener. The following quote reflects another survivor's recognition of her victimization, and her need for transcendence:

When I knew what was going on in my, in that relationship, when it actually dawned on me, that his hitting me wasn't suppose to happen, I tried to think about ways to get out of—ways to make it stop. Not ways to leave the marriage, but I thought—if I told people, that would do it.

This quote reflects the narrator's reconceptualization of her experience, a time when she realized that complacency regarding the abuse was no longer acceptable. This marked the beginning of her transcendence, the initial recognition of the need for change.

As the narrator ascends to a higher level of transcendence, the narrators' expressions include descriptions of periods of struggle. This struggle involves moving beyond initial realization of the need for personal transcendence, to enacting the change needed for further development. One narrator expresses her simultaneous feelings of fear and anger, which became a necessary struggle for her to endure, to become further empowered:

So he shot this man in a bar, this is what I know. And, Lori, you know, I was scared, but I was also very indignant and pissed off about this. And, it's kind of a dichotomy, because I, for years, was such a wuss, and then, like this (she marks a hard slap sound), I'm empowered, and I move out. And, I'm yes, I am in hiding, but all of a sudden I'm feeling, this isn't right, this isn't fair, I don't want to do this.

Ascending from such a struggle as a more independent individual, is an important step in continued transformation performance. Narrating one's experience becomes a way of giving meaning to past experience, and giving plausibility to future performances of empowerment. Sullivan Norton (1989) explains:

Telling a story organizes an individual's impressions of experience. Consider the impulse to bear witness, which characterizes and motivates survivors of devastating events and personal tragedies. The urge to speak out about the tragedy helps the survivor extract significance from absurdity and meaning from meaninglessness. Without the story, there is nothing on which to stand, no context from which to organize meaning. By telling the story, one organizes meaning in a way that makes it possible to cope with what happened (p. 183–184).

By witnessing about their experience, the narrators reinforce their triumph over the obstacles they faced as they emerged to an empowered status. Such a rendering highlights the change which occurs in the lives of victims who became survivors. Richard Schechner (1977) distinguishes his notion of transformation from Victor Turner's notion that life-dramas facilitate conflict resolution:

Turner locates the essential drama in conflict and conflict resolution. I locate it in transformation in using theatre as a way to experiment with or act out and ratify change. Transformations in theatre occur in three different places, and at three different levels: (1) in the drama, that is, the story; (2) in the performers whose special task it is to temporarily undergo a rearrangement of their body/mind; (3) in the audience where changes may either by temporary (entertainment) or permanent (ritual) (p. 123).

The narrators for this study used the act of telling as a means to perpetuate further change in their lives, in a similar way to that described by Schechner (1977). Schechner's (1977) notion that performers "temporarily undergo a rearrangement of their body/mind" (p. 123), seems quite true regarding the telling of survivor narratives. Telling survivor narratives allows the narrators to position themselves positively and envision themselves as sustaining independent lives in the future, free from the hold or control of their abusers. This is consistent with Kerby's (1991) notion that "the stories we tell are part and parcel of our becoming. They are a mode of vision, plotting what is good and what is bad for us, what is possible, and what is not—plotting who we may become" (p. 54). Additionally, Polkinghorne (1988) contends that "we achieve our personal identities and self concept through use of narrative configuration, and make our existence into a whole by understanding it as an expression of a single, unfolding story" (p. 150). Such a use of narrative configuration is reflected in the following excerpt in which the narrator discusses alternative ways of dealing with her abuse:

I didn't want anybody to know what he was doing. I wanted to let them think our relationship was going so good, we didn't have want for nothing. But inside I was dying—wanted to kill myself, maybe things would be better if I wasn't alive. And I thought about the kids, that stopped me. I ain't gonna say right now my world revolves around my kids, but it's now—I do care about myself. I had to learn, hey, you're not a bad person—you're a good person. I'm what they call a survivor—and I'm gonna survive. I don't need a man to tell me this.

This quote marks a transitory point for this narrator. She explains how she moved from silence about her abuse, which left her with thoughts of suicide, to a more empowered position as a person who defines herself as a survivor. This excerpt marks a period when this survivor, who just recently removed herself from her abusive relationship, labels herself as a survivor. The articulated re/expression of her desire and belief that she will "survive," emphasizes the transitory power of projecting a positive future story on facilitating such a change. By eventually telling others about the abuse, this narrator was able to break the pretense surrounding her marriage, that is, to stop covering up the abuse, and receive help from a social network. Although she is only recently separated from her abuser, she envisions or recasts herself as a survivor. This envisioning is facilitated by the narrative act. It was through personal storytelling that she gained access to Haven House. It is through narration that she is encouraged by the staff, and is able to work through some of her own thoughts and feelings about her abuse, and plan for her future. Once again, as Jean-Paul Sartre wrote, "each one, by reinventing his own issue, invents himself. Man must be invented each day" (p. 3). Through each performance of their personal stories of abuse, the narrators actively reinvent themselves. Using the narrative act is an important way in which the narrators set the stage for recollections of past transcendence, as well as setting goals for their future.

DISCUSSION

Invoking performance strategies in the telling of abuse survivor narratives becomes an important way in which narrators can position themselves and others in the telling, construct a convincing story line, and set the stage for past and future transformation from victimization to survivorship. Through effective storytelling performances, the narrators were able to gain access to a shelter, support from family and friends, and achieve personal empowerment through personal reflection. Robinson (1981) contends that "telling stories about personal experience is a prominent part of everyday discourse, and competence in such narration is an essential skill for members of a speech community" (p. 58). Such competence is vitally important to survivors of abuse. The narrators for this study exhibited such performance competence. My thoughts continue to wander to those who cannot tell, or cannot convince others of their plight, will they ever be able to perform survivor? Performative features allow transcendence to occur, to be realized and to be pointed to in the performance and re-performance of abuse survivor narratives.

Chapter Five

Understanding Personal Narratives Through Re-Performance

INTRODUCTION

In November 1993, a production entitled, "Breaking the Cycle" was staged in the Marion Kleinau Theatre of Southern Illinois University in Carbondale, Illinois. "Breaking the Cycle" is a one act show in which excerpts of abuse survivor narratives, poetry, and feminist theory are juxtaposed to create a one hour performance. The show begins with an empty chair, dimly lit on stage. The voice of an absent woman fills the performance space via a voice-over, as she recounts her struggle in an abusive relationship. A central narrator emerges from the audience, and begins to recount her past experiences of abuse. Unable to continue, she relinquishes the performance space to other characters on stage. At this point, the central narrator's "journey" begins. Her journey is a transformation from victimization to empowerment. Throughout the production, the central narrator becomes privy to the survival stories of other characters. These characters represent voices of other survivors of domestic violence and abuse. Initially, she is unable to interact with the other characters. However, by listening to them, and coming to understand their experiences, she is able to reconceptualize her own incidents of abuse, and gradually piece together her own survivor narrative.

During the second half of the show, the characters on stage are able to interact. Their perceptions and detailed recountings are juxtaposed to serve as commentary on the issues of domestic violence and abuse. Eventually, the central narrator comes to reconceptualize her experiences as those of victimization. This revelation is important, because it allows her to shift away from victim blame, and openly narrate her life story.

Throughout the production, moments occur when the central narrator retreats from her newly gained empowered status. Yet, every time she recovers from

96

these moments, she further validates her survivorship. Near the close of the show, the characters emerge to varying degrees of empowerment. The production closes with the voice of an unidentified woman, symbolized once again by the empty chair, who continues to be trapped in a cycle of violence. Her narrative represents the struggle that many abuse victims continually endure.

The production process for "Breaking the Cycle" began as an attempt to explore abuse victims' transformation to abuse survivors, as facilitated by the act of narrating their experiences of abuse. Specifically, the assistant director, Christine Broda-Bahm, and I sought to examine the connection, if any, which existed between narrative performance and teller empowerment.

Our pre-production decisions were guided by four primary assumptions, (1) that a re-performance of the personal narratives of abuse survivors could advance a greater understanding of the experience of survivors; (2) that such a performance could be managed with a realistic commitment of accountability to the others represented in the performance; (3) that staging such narratives could be meaningful to those involved in the show as well as meaningful to the audience, because of the power of performance, and (4) that staging the narratives could generate a greater sense of knowing than another form of research. We used these assumptions, as we formed and approached the performance objectives for "Breaking the Cycle." In the following section, the performance objectives for "Breaking the Cycle" will be discussed.

PERFORMANCE OBJECTIVES

Several performance objectives were sought during the process of staging "Breaking the Cycle." The objectives of this production included promoting inclusivity, an expression of common themes, implicating the audience, preserving the teller's voice and exploring the connection between narrative performance and teller empowerment.

Inclusivity

One primary objective for this production was to give presence to many different stories of survival. We pursued inclusivity, after a preliminary analysis of the narratives suggested a blurring of the lines which separate different types of abuse. For example, many narratives of spousal battery yielded discussions of prior incidents of molestation or rape. While the abusive incidents recounted were often dissimilar in kind, the informants expressed similar coping strategies which they invoked as they transcended from victim to survivor. For example, they described shifting blame away from themselves, pursuing alternative roles in their life world, and so forth, as ways of coping with their

past experiences. Consequently, many different types of survivors were represented on stage, including survivors of battery, incest and acquaintance rape.
In addition, a variety of abusive relationships were staged, including father-
son, daughter-father, spousal and acquaintance relationships. This scripting
choice was applied in an effort to demonstrate the widest possible representation of experiences found in the narratives collected for this study.

In addition to promoting inclusivity by offering diverse narrative recountings of abuse, we sought inclusivity in casting decisions as well. For example, we sought to include cast members who represented demographic diversity in the categories of age, sex, race, and socio-economic class. We did not
attempt to cast the performers in these categories to mirror the informants'
personal demographics, necessarily. Instead, we hoped to offer inclusivity
which mirrored the demographic background of our audience. We did not, for
example, want the show to be entirely devoted to the victimization of women,
or reflect one socio-economic group of individuals. Consequently, the cast
consisted of six performers, approximately 18–35 years of age. Performers
included two African American women, two white women, and two white
men, of various socio-economic backgrounds. Additionally, the woman who
narrates via a voice-over is staged to represent "every woman." However, efforts to be inclusive were somewhat constrained by the population of performers who auditioned for the show.

Expression of Common Themes

When gathering material for the show, I examined various sources of survival
stories. Much of the performance text came from excerpts of interviews I conducted with abuse survivors. Additionally, material included narratives collected by NiCarthy (1987), printed in her book, "The One's Who Got Away,"
as well as narratives cited in a government report on domestic violence and
abuse (United States Commission on Civil Rights, 1978). Also scripted was
poetry, including May Swenson's "Bleeding," which served as a poignant
metaphor for violence and abuse, and Marge Piercy's "Rape Poem." Finally,
I included feminist theory, according to Dworkin (1987), regarding the performance of gender roles and patriarchy in the dominant culture. An analysis
of this material yielded common themes of "survivor discourse," including
references to experiencing an initial sense of culpability, isolation, and de-
spair regarding victimization, which eventually evolved into feelings of personal empowerment. Consequently, a second performance objective was our
attempt to highlight these common themes throughout the performances.

The performers, directors and audience for this production were given access to the life world of survivors of domestic violence and abuse through the

re-performance of the survivor narratives. During the four-week rehearsal process, participants in the production became immersed in the life world of these narrators. Through analysis and discussion of these common themes contained in the narratives, the directors and cast were able to understand experiences of victimization and empowerment more completely. Understanding the common threads of experience became an important way for the performers to access the voices of the informants, and pursue embodiment of the characters represented in the text.

Implicating the Audience

The audiences for this production included two primary groups. One audience, who viewed the production at the Marion Kleinau Theatre, included faculty and students of Southern Illinois University, as well as some members of the local community. Another group audienced the performance at Purdue University Calumet, in Hammond, Indiana. Members of this audience also included faculty and students, as well as guest respondents from local shelters for victims of domestic violence. Because of the prevalence of abuse within our culture, it is safe to assume that many of our audience members had either experienced or observed violence or abuse at some point in their lives. Therefore, the audiences most likely included victims, survivors and abusive individuals.

During the development of the performance material, we were concerned with constructing ways to position the audience during the subsequent re-performance of the survivor narratives. Our hope was to position the audience in two ways. First, we wanted them to empathize with the narrators' stories of victimization and survivorship. In that sense, the audience could imaginatively locate themselves on stage, by sharing the narrators' stories, as a set of common experiences. Additionally, and perhaps more importantly, we attempted to implicate the audience in the perpetuation of abuse, by highlighting an individual's potential complacency. For example, by accepting traditional patriarchal roles and/or accepting the public-private sphere distinction regarding intimate disclosure, people may be complicit in preventing victims from reporting their abuse in the public sector.

Preserving the Teller's Voice

Narrating one's experiences of victimization is not always easy. Yet, through such narration, important information regarding the victim's life world and transcendence to survivorship is often highlighted and explored. This production emerged from an interest in better understanding how victims and survivors work through the performance of everyday life. Informants report being complacent in their past performance of traditional roles. Performance of traditional roles can involve conformity to socially accepted behaviors and cultural objectives which preserve patriarchy, such as submission to male dominance and hierarchies of power distribution. Such submission is further manifested and perpetuated by incidents of domestic violence and abuse.

Accessibility to survivor narratives is somewhat limited, partly due to the suppression of voices of victims and survivors promoted by the dominant culture. In Chapter One, I described a variety of factors which influence the telling of survivor narratives. These include the willingness and ability of the narrator to describe his or her experience, the public-private sphere distinction which restricts open disclosure, and the narrator's perceived threat of injury or loss (which may be compounded by the act of telling). The informants for this production confronted such factors (which suppress the voices of survivors), prior to their telling. Consequently, they incurred potentially high costs of telling when they agreed to be interviewed. Recognizing the costs of telling that the survivors may have incurred through the original performance of their narratives, prompted us to handle the narratives collected for this production with care and sensitivity. For example, when juxtapositioning various performance material, the adaptor/director confronts certain risks. One risk is distorting the original teller's ideas by recontextualizing the material during re-performance. Another risk is appropriating the original teller's perspective by making it subordinate to the adaptor/director's voice. To avoid such risks, we made a conscious attempt to highlight the informants' perspectives, and not deliberately manipulate their perspectives for our own service, for example, because it would be more aesthetically powerful if the informant's perspective was usurped. Above all, was our effort to secure narrator confidentiality and preserve the original teller's voice.

Accountability to the Other

During the process of interviewing, the script compilation, and throughout the rehearsal process and final performances, ethical questions and moral challenges emerged. For example, we questioned, how can we ensure accountability to the other? What are the specific consequences of staging narratives of abuse survivors? What happens when the material generated is potentially damaging to the tellers? What are the consequences of working with such material on the performers and audience? Of primary significance was the question of whether it was ethical to use such intimate material at all, that is, is it "right" to put on display, the most intimate details of these peoples' lives? Robinson (1981) explains that, "experiences of victimization have an ambivalent status as candidates for narration . . . characteristically, such experiences produce shame, anger, often guilt in the victim, and are regarded as secrets rather than stories to tell" (p. 63). Further, Langellier (1989) contends that when disclosing intimate personal narratives, "the teller's risk being misunderstood, personally disliked, or socially ostracized" (p. 257). Consequently, early in the process, important questions of accountability to the other in re-performance of abuse survivor narratives shaped the production concept. Conquergood's (1985) discussion of dialogic performance offers important insight on how to promote accountability to the other. Conquergood asserts that unethical performance stances should be avoided when engaging the other through performance. These unethical stances include (1) "the Custodian's rip off," when "a strong attraction to the other coupled with extreme detachment results in acquisitiveness instead of genuine inquiry, plunder more than performance" (p. 5); (2) the "enthusiasts infatuation," when "too facile identification with the other coupled with enthusiastic commitment produces naïve and glib performances marked by superficiality" (p. 6); (3) the "Curator's exhibitionism," "whereas the enthusiast assumed too easily an Identity with the other, the curator is committed to the Difference of the other" (p. 7); and (4) the "Skeptic's cop out," those "refuge of cowards and cynics," who "instead of facing up to struggling with the ethical tensions and moral ambiguities of performing culturally sensitive material," do not attempt such performances (p. 8). Conquergood (1985) suggests engaging in a dialogical performance with the other. He explains:

> This performative stance struggles to bring together different voices, world views, value systems and beliefs so that they can have a conversation with one another. The aim of dialogical performance is to bring self and other together so that they can question, debate and challenge one another (p. 9)

Consequently, engaging in a dialogical performance between the cast and informants for this production became a primary rehearsal objective used to insure greater accountability to the other represented in the performance text. Our belief was, by participating in a dialogical performance approach, we could pursue accountability to the other (characters represented in the performance text), more successfully. During private conversations I had with cast members at various times during the rehearsal process, I learned that some performers struggled with ethical dilemmas which kept them from achieving a dialogical relationship with their characters, for some time. For example, in a post-performance taped narrative, one performer reported feeling, "My God, this is a real woman's words, who am I to take this woman's most tragic part of her entire existence and put it on public display?" Similarly, another performer disclosed that he questioned the overall motives of the production, for example, was the production beneficial to abuse survivors, "I felt as if there was some dishonesty there, some insincerity there . . . my reaction was to say, this performance isn't about them at all. It is about me." Attitudes such as those represented in the performer's quotes, seem similar to what Conquergood (1985) labels, the "skeptic's cop out," that is, their doubts about being able to confront the ethical challenges resulted in a belief that they could not participate in a dialogical relationship with their characters. In his taped narrative, a performer claimed, "I found myself rehearsing in a detached manner. . . . It was as if I didn't want to let go and allow myself to feel the emotions of the character during rehearsal," yet, this same performer noted that "There have been people in my life who have suffered abuse, and I wanted to empathize with them." This represents a struggle the performers encountered during rehearsal. It is a struggle between empathy with their characters and detachment, as they tried to deal with their attitudes and experiences regarding the sensitive material contained in the performance text. Through continued rehearsal, the performers reported achieving a "conversation" with their characters, which allowed them to merge or closely align themselves with their characters. As directors, we faced concerns over accountability to the other as well. We resisted the unethical stances which Conquergood (1985) labels, the "custodian's rip off" and the "enthusiast's infatuation." We did not want to become so detached from the material that we could not pursue "genuine inquiry" into our research objectives. Yet, we were careful not to produce a superficial representation of abuse survivors and their stories. Consequently, we kept the survivors' stories at the center of our discussion. We wanted the voices of the informants to guide our work, so that we would not lose sight of our performance objectives. Additionally, we tried to respect the informants' ownership of their life stories. In our work with survivor narratives, self reflexivity as well as group reflexivity (as we helped each other keep our common goals in check) became important ways for us to ensure accountability to the other more completely.

Narrative Performance and Teller Empowerment

Perhaps one of the most significant objectives of this production was to increase our understanding of the potential connection between narrative performance and teller empowerment. In an effort to discern the significance of such a connection, we examined the survivor narratives on three primary levels, (1) we analyzed the narratives to find possible instances where the informants alluded to or acknowledged a link between narrative performance and empowerment; (2) we assessed the outcome of the interview sessions, as potentially empowering or disempowering experiences, and; (3) we examined the results of how the discourse of the informants shaped the ways in which the performers positioned the informants on stage. Throughout the production process, our work was guided by the notion that the re-performance of a personal narrative, particularly an abuse survivor narrative, is empowering to the original teller.

The performance and re-performance of survivor narratives seems to serve as an important means for the teller to transcend to survivor, to become empowered. An analysis of the narratives collected for the show suggests that the narrators are empowered by their authority to tell "their stories." By re-performing their narratives, they are able to determine the narrative construction and performance strategies they will invoke. As I mentioned in Chapter Four, the narrators are able to position themselves in empowered statuses. Such empowerment can be witnessed in the re-performance of the survivor stories in a theatrically-framed environment as well. The performers in "Breaking the cycle," seemed to sense the notion of empowerment, as it occurred in the telling. They positioned their characters in similar ways that the informants positioned themselves in the interview performances. For example, at moments when the informants positioned themselves in powerful statuses, the performers' stances, posture and demeanor reflected confidence and empowerment.

Richardson (1990) contends that "narration displays the goals and intentions of human actors . . . it allows us to contemplate the effects of our actions, and alter the directions of our lives" (p. 177). Richardson (1990) further explains that "people organize their personal biographies and understand them through the stories they create to explain and justify their experience . . . social and generational cohesion, as well as social change, depend on the ability to empathize with the life stories of others" (p. 126–127). Similarly, Turner (1982) contends, that "there must be a dialectic between performing and learning. One learns through performing, then performs the understanding so gained" (p. 94). In an effort to understand the abuse survivor narratives more fully, to empathize with the informants, and gain understanding through re-performance, we pursued our performance objectives strategically. In the section which follows, I will describe the scripting and staging choices we made to achieve our performance objectives.

PURSUING PERFORMANCE OBJECTIVES

To meet the objectives set for this production, we invoked certain choices regarding scripting and staging the material. Scripting the material involved selecting an organizing principal which could frame the show. The organizing

principal invoked was used to help guide the audience through their performance. We wanted to use the organizing principal to facilitate greater audience
empathy and understanding, as well as provide continuity to the production.
Additionally, careful consideration was given to staging the material to highlight theoretical issues surrounding abuse within the performance text. Finally, we attempted to account for those who remain victims of abuse, those
who have not yet transcended to survivors.

Responding Personally to the Script-in-Progress

Compiling the informants' stories, poetry and feminist theory in a meaningful and coherent way, represented one struggle I confronted when scripting
"Breaking the Cycle." Another struggle emerged as I attempted to provide an
organizing principal for the performance text. The script for "Breaking the
Cycle" was divided into nine scenes and ran approximately one hour in
length. The scenes were divided thematically and generally involved a juxtapositioning of the different narratives and poems collected, in conversation
with, or commenting upon each other.

Initially, I envisioned a compilation of many self-contained performances
within the hour-long performance of the show. I had not believed that transi-
tions between the narratives were necessary. Yet, I knew that I wanted to
highlight the victims' move to survivorship in the production. I realized that
an organizing principal was necessary to offer continuity to the performance
text, which could make the show more understandable and meaningful to the
audience. However, after transcribing and compiling the material for the
show, I experienced difficulty in organizing the material into such an under-
standable, meaningful text. I felt as if I had personally shut down, that issues
from my past created a barrier that prevented the completion of the script. I
had become resistant to the material. As I pursued completion of this project,
I had conversations with Dr. Carol Benton, of Central Missouri State University, who has experience working with intimate narrative performances. She
asked me to describe my reasons for engaging in this particular production
process, and how it had informed the decisions I had made in preparation for
the show. As I described my involvement and the evolution of my understanding regarding abuse, transformation and empowerment, she pointed out
that by suppressing my own feelings regarding past experiences in my life, I
was unable to continue developing the production. She suggested that I au-
diotape a narrative of my own past experiences for possible inclusion in the
show. Initially, I found this notion problematic. I didn't want this to be a show
about me. I wanted to highlight the experiences of other survivors, to accom-
plish the original objectives set forth for this production. I examined my mo-

tives for invoking such a project in the first place. I did not want the show to develop into a cathartic experience pursued for my own satisfaction or benefit. Yet, I could no longer access the voices of the narrators I interviewed without acknowledging my own feelings. I believe now that I needed to validate my experience in order to collaborate with the other voices represented in the narratives.

When I finally did narrate my experience, I found that my perceptions regarding abuse had changed. I found that listening to the narratives of others, and working with the issues of domestic violence and abuse, allowed me to understand my past experiences more completely. I had come to understand victimization and abuse personally, through the research process. This understanding was reflected in my narrative. Consequently, (at Carol Benton's suggestion), I decided to use my narrative as the central organizing narrative for the show. My narrative was now framed as a woman's journey of discovery, "my own" journey of understanding. This narrator would weave her experience in and out of the lives of other survivors represented on stage. As she becomes privy to their stories, she gradually is able to reconceptualize her own experience. She then becomes educated (as I had been educated) regarding victimization and survivorship in a manner similar (parallel) to that put forth for the audience's experience with the other compiled material. My anonymity was preserved throughout the rehearsal process and performances of "Breaking the Cycle," with the exception of my "confession" to the assistant director, approximately mid-point in the rehearsal process. Staging my narrative became an alternative means of voicing my story.

STAGING THE PERFORMANCE TEXT

After scripting decisions were implemented, decisions regarding how to stage the material arose. We wanted to highlight the significance of patriarchy on domestic violence and abuse, and stage the hierarchies which are embedded in abusive relationships. Additionally, we wanted to highlight the victims and survivors feelings and emotions regarding their involvement in abusive relationships. In this section, I will discuss the methods we used to stage patriarchy and hierarchies, as well as how we employed minimal context to highlight the victim's experience.

Theoretical Issues: Performing Patriarchy

Alexander, Moore and Alexander (1991) found that, in heterosexual couples where the male held conservative-traditional views and the female more liberal views, the "enculturation of patriarchal values does seem to have an impact on the increased likelihood of violence" (p. 666). In addition, Hutchings (1988) contends that society, which is guided by the dominant culture, "conveys messages, images, as to what a woman should be and what a man should be. This image reduces a woman to a secondary position and causes her to devalue herself" (p. 21). As described in Chapter One, such behavioral, or role-oriented constraints may restrict the victim's willingness to seek help through narration. Within a patriarchal society which promotes ideals such as gender-specific behaviors, i.e., dominance and submission, a female may not seek help because she has labeled herself as the "fault" of her abusive experiences, or she may feel that she has no recourse due to her lack of status within society. A male victim may not seek help because of the stigma of male dominance and power which is perpetuated by patriarchy. He may remain silent for fear of rejection, chastisement, or fear or failure. Consequently, if an abuse victim deviates from the values perpetuated by patriarchy, she or he may be subjected to increased abuse. Alexander et al. (1991) also maintain, "researchers have indeed discovered that abusive men frequently espouse more traditional views about women than non-abusive men" (p. 658). If these traditional views are shared by the victim, they may limit the victim's perception of alternative performative possibilities and may cause him or her to believe the abuse is his or her own fault. An internalization of fault may result in silence on the part of the victim. This silence may further perpetuate the abusive incidents. A preliminary analysis of the narratives collected for "Breaking the Cycle" demonstrated feelings of submission and isolation on the part of the victim. Staging choices were made based on the hierarchical relationships which were indicated in the narratives. In the next section, I will discuss the various staging choices we employed to represent patriarchy and hierarchies in the production.

Staging Hierarchies

Hierarchical relationships were evidenced in narratives of women who were victimized by men as well as children (who are now adults) who were victimized by adults who held "higher" positions of dominance in their lives. In an effort to represent the hierarchical relationships on stage, the set for this production consisted of various levels, stairs and platforms. In moments where the "victim" and "abuser" were staged simultaneously, the "victim" was placed on lower set areas. Additionally, the central narrator, who listened to the others' survival stories, gradually ascended from body positions on the floor to higher levels represented by the stairs stage center. This was not done in a linear fashion, however, when moments of her regression to victimization occurred, the narrator was placed in lower positions of authority. Ultimately, the survivors were placed at various levels of symbolically empowered positions at the conclusion of the show, indicating the daily struggles experienced by abuse victims and survivors.

Minimizing Context

In their narrative discourse, informants described feelings of isolation from friends, family, and other support systems, when they were involved in abusive relationships. In an effort to highlight these feelings of isolation, we employed minimal contextual frames. For example, early narrators who often spoke as if in the same scene with the abuser, sat alone, isolated, unable to interact with the central narrator, although she was privy to their experiences. As the show progressed, the narrators were able to interact, although an effort was made to disguise any "real" attempt to contextualize the re-tellings in a manner which may have accompanied the original telling of the narrative. This choice, to privilege the sense of isolation over context was not without costs. The telling of personal narratives is influenced by the cultural context in which the telling occurs. Rules, roles and performance expectations help determine how the narrative is constructed and how it is received by members of a given society. Bauman (1986) notes that, "oral performance, like all human activity is situated, its form, meaning, and functions rooted in culturally defined scenes or events—bounded segments of the flow of behavior and experience that constitute meaningful experience contexts for action, interpretation, and evaluation" (p. 3). Rules governing human communication such as "appropriateness" of topic, occasion, setting and the relationship of the interactants all impact the performance of narratives in everyday life. Langellier (1989) contends that, "like all performance events, personal narrative is structured by the culture in which it operates. The performance approach attempts to index the ground rules constraining performance, for example, genre, shared social attributes and cultural values and speech situation" (p. 255–256). This is consistent with Bakhtin's notion of "heteroglossia," which suggests "at any given time, in any given place, there will be a set of conditions . . . that will insure that a word uttered in that place and at that time will have a meaning different than it would have under any other conditions" (Holoquist, 1981, p. 423). Consequently, by eliminating original contextual features (which would have been impossible to fully recapture in any case), and replacing the context with on-stage isolation, the re-performance has lost important dimensions of the original telling. Some of the loses include the dynamics of the teller-listener interaction, the original performance features, and perhaps most importantly, a demonstration of the survivor's decision to disclose.

First, as I described in Chapter One, the teller-listener interaction plays a significant part in narrative construction. Mandelbaum (1989) describes a listener as a "co-author" of a narrated story. She contends that "recipients have resources with which they may actually initiate and work through with the teller, a change in the nature of storytelling, while the storytelling is in progress" (p. 114). When we made the decision to "isolate" the cast members as they re-performed the narrative text, we did so in an effort to highlight the sense of isolation that victims of abuse often report. We did not wish to re-enact the interview (original) performance during this production, however, by minimizing context, and not placing an "intended" receiver/listener on stage, we lost an important part of the original performance of the text. We lost the sense that the narratives were co-produced and facilitated by the interaction between narrator and narratee. Without placing the listener on stage, we required the audience to fill-in-the-gaps regarding the "intended" receiver of the message. Consequently, we may have lost insight into how narratives are co-produced. Rehearsing the teller-listener interaction may have offered insight into the dynamics of such a relationship, and its relative influence on the narrative event.

Second, on-stage isolation and minimal context results in a loss of performance features which accompanied the original performance of the text. For example, the performers were not allowed the luxury of narrating in a realistic environment, using similar furniture or props. They were given only chairs, blocks or platforms from which to tell their characters' stories. The informants' original performance features sometimes included such behaviors as hugging or caressing their children as they described how the child gave them strength to leave an abusive mate. Such behaviors could not be re-performed using isolation and minimal context. Seating positions, use of space, and so forth, were constrained during the re-performance due to performance-space boundaries. Consequently, such contextual frames were housed in the imaginations of the performers and transferred to the audience not in a realistic way, such as through mimesis or re-enactment, where performers use props and settings which mirror those of the original telling, but symbolically, through the absence of everyday objects, environments and so forth.

Finally, one of the most significant loses which resulted during the re-performance, were details surrounding the survivors' decisions to disclose. Fine and Speer (1977) contend that "the structure of the performance event itself may be emergent, since the act sequence of the event and/or the ground rules of performance may shift as they are negotiated by performer and audience in a dynamic relationship" (p. 378). During the interview sessions which resulted in performance material for "Breaking the Cycle," the survivors chose to disclose based on the dynamics of the teller-listener relationship. The setting, the participants' roles in the interaction, and the interaction itself facilitated the telling. By using minimal context, the survivors' decisions to tell could not be explored as fully through the rehearsal and performance of the text. Hence, information regarding the contexts which facilitated the decision to tell may not have been made explicit in the re-performances of the narratives. Despite the loses incurred, isolation and minimum context serve as important strategies to highlight the experiences of victimization and abuse.

Representing the Victim

Another staging choice involved representing those abuse victims who had not yet experienced a transformation to survivorship. Those victims were represented by the voice of a woman, who recounts her experience via a voice-over in the theatre. An empty chair on stage is used to symbolize her isolation and invisibility from society. She represents those individuals who continue to be trapped in a cycle of violence. Her narrative opens and closes the show. Her presence was designed as a way of implicating the audience, that is, to bring to their attention the fact that many individuals, possibly including members of the audience, remain trapped in silence. This message was constructed to educate all audiences of the narratives on our own individual responsibility of promoting patriarchy and silence, which ultimately perpetuates abuse.

PERFORMANCE AND RE-PERFORMANCE: AREAS OF CONVERGENCE AND PERFORMANCE KNOWLEDGE GAINED

The performance and re-performance of abuse survivor narratives rely on similar performative strategies and performance features. For example, both the informants and stage performers attempt to create believable characters and a convincing story line. Although the stage performers work from a prepared text, their task of promoting believability is shared by the original narrators (as they prepared the text for performance and eventual re-performance). Both the original tellers and the stage performers sought to increase audience understanding and empathy. Strategies engaged to evoke such empathy include such features as dramatic emphasis, vocal inflection and intonation, sincerity of the speaker, and so forth.

Although the contexts of the telling differed significantly, the performances invoked by the original narrators and the stage performers were more similar than dissimilar. For example, individuals who seek admission into a shelter, such as Haven House, utilize personal embodiment of their narratives as they recount details of their experience to a counseling coordinator or another member of the staff, who must decide whether an individual is indeed a victim who is entitled to services at the shelter. Once an individual gains access to the shelter, her story experiences a certain disembodiment as one staff member recounts the client's experience on paper, or to another member of the staff. Or, perhaps a friend or family member seeks assistance from the staff on behalf of the victim. Despite the disembodied nature of the narrative discourse, the life of the narrative is perpetuated. Re-performance of the narrative is yet another example of how the life of a narrative is propelled. In a sense, the staged performance is not entirely different than the life dramas from which the text is drawn, that is, the original performance. Hence, the narrative seems to have a life of its own. Obviously, objectives for narrative performance and re-performance can differ significantly. For example, an original narrator may be seeking life sustaining assistance, whereas a stage performer may be seeking an aesthetically compelling performance. Yet, when one views the stage as an alternative discourse field, the objectives appear more closely aligned. The original performers and stage performers utilize the same performance text, invoke similar performative strategies, and seek similar audience responses.

What, then, can be gained through staging abuse survivor narratives? For the stage performers, embodiment of the narratives offered direct personal access to the other in their performances. In post-performance reflections regarding the production process, some performers reported experiencing unique connections to the original tellers which varied in intensity. For example, one performer indicated a very strong connection with her "character" as she became absorbed in the discourse of the narrative. Her connection with the original teller was emphasized by the similarities in experiences of past abuse that they shared, as well as the steps they invoked to move toward survivorship. At times, some of the performers became so closely aligned with their characters' experiences, that they expressed concerns about engaging fully embodied performances. One performer expressed a fear of "losing it" during a performance. For example, she believed that she may become overly emotional herself and not be able to continue performing. Another explained how he held back from fully portraying his character until the opening performance, because of fear regarding the emotional pain that such a performance could invoke. Other performers, however, reported approaching their "characters" just as they might have any "fictive" character in any performance.

As the director/compiler, my experience was quite different. I could witness the response of the performers to the material, but not fully engage it. One way in which I measured the performance and it's relative impact on the cast and audience was through the discussion sessions which followed performances at the Marion Kleinau Theatre and Purdue Calumet. Although the two audiences were similar, both performance settings were on university campuses with faculty and students in attendance, the audiencing objectives pursued by the two audiences seemed quite different. The objectives became apparent in the post-performance discussion sessions.

The discussion following a performance at the Kleinau Theatre focused significantly on the performance choices made and how such choices promoted the research agenda. Christine Broda-Bahm (1994) explains the focus of the Kleinau discussion led by Carol Benton:

> We identified two emergent themes within the critique period. The first theme dealt with the search for conceptualization. The audience raised issues about inclusiveness of our conception of abuse, but also voiced concern over the exclusiveness of the instances of abuse utilized. The second emergent theme is the search for proscriptives. The audience raised issues pertaining to the appropriate actions to be taken in order to move toward becoming a "survivor" as well as issues pertaining to the category of "survivorship" and characteristics indicative of such individuals (p. 19)

By emphasizing the need to be located on stage, the audience reinforced our initial belief that such inclusivity would be an important means by which to achieve audience empathy. The audience expressed a desire to be included in the stage representations of abuse. The implications of such a response on the audiencing of abuse survivor narratives in general are significant, in that, audience members seem to search for commonalities in the experience between the narratee and themselves. They search for identifiable themes which are consistent with their own images of what victimization and survivorship look like or sound like. Because of such constructed images, survivors seem required to reinforce the listener's images in their narrative discourse. To reinforce these images, then, survivors must construct their narratives strategically in order to achieve "victim status." In the absence of such details or performative strategies, the story line becomes less convincing, and perhaps, assistance to the survivor may be harder to achieve.

The second focus of the Kleinau post-performance discussion, that is, the need for the audience to define the labels, characteristics, and methods, seems to be an attempt by the audience to "fit" the survivors into socially constructed ideals consistent with their own predetermined categories. What emerged from this line of discussion was reinforcement of the notion that victimization and survivorship are determined by degrees that exist on a continuum, that individuals who represent victims and survivors do not fit into dichotomous categories that are neatly distinguishable entities.

The discussion session which followed the performance at Purdue Calumet was quite different. With many self-admitted survivors in the audience at Purdue, the discussion focused initially on believability. Like the Kleinau audience, the Purdue audience suggested that they were able to identify with the performances on stage, which consequently made the performances "believable" for them. The focus quickly changed as the discussion turned to attribution of blame for incidents of domestic violence and abuse. With a predominantly female configuration of the Purdue audience, the audience's responses often attributed blame to men, social service providers (mostly men) and religious hierarchies (predominately run by male clergy). However, some comments, even from admitted survivors, were indicative of victim blame, such as, "if she had only . . . he wouldn't have been able to continue abusing her," and so forth. In a sense, the Purdue performance seemed like a catalyst for a survivor "pep rally" of sorts. That is, it turned into a means for survivors to "bond" with one another as they contributed to the "collective story" (Richardson, 1990) represented on stage.

Witnessing the differing audience responses reinforced the significance of the teller-listner interaction in facilitating teller empowerment or potential disempowerment. The diversity of the audience responses raises important questions regarding the performance and re-performance of survivor narratives. For example, when victims of abuse narrate their experiences, what are the consequences of unsympathetic listener responses? Must a survivor construct a narrative so that it remains consistent with the listener's image of abuse to be afforded the label of survivor? How do victims and survivors audience their own experiences of victimization? How many victims remain silenced because they do not conform to socially constructed images of victim performance?

Perhaps the greatest lesson learned from staging "Breaking the cycle" came from the inclusion of my own life story in the performance text. While both the assistant director and I have experienced violence or abuse in past relationships, we did not address these experiences with the cast during the rehearsal or performances of the show, we didn't address this fact in our initial discussions of production concept or production process. A few persons working on the show alluded to past experiences of victimization, two during pre-production discussions with me, the other, at the Kleinau post-performance discussion. Other cast members openly articulated their feelings and opinions regarding the issues of domestic violence and abuse, but did not directly state a personal connection to abusive experiences. A cast member who disclosed personal information to me prior to the rehearsal process, learned, in part, of my past experiences. However, we did not openly discuss my past during the rehearsal process. In a sense, our failure to disclose openly with the cast seems questionable ethically. Yet, our lack of disclosure seemed justified (at least I believed that to be the case, as one of our foremost performance objectives was to highlight the informants' experiences, not to (intentionally) use the rehearsal and performance process for personal healing). Our research objective was to assess the correlation between narrative performance and teller empowerment. If telling yields empowerment, we must ask ourselves why we did not engage in open telling with others involved in the show. Perhaps the show served as an alternative means by which to stage our perceptions of our experiences. The inclusion of my story represented tapping into an alternative discourse space. As with the other narrators' voices included in the performance, I remained anonymous. As I witnessed the performance and rehearsal process surrounding my own narrative, I began to question the primary assumptions of my research. If telling is empowering, why didn't I feel empowered? Witnessing the rehearsal of my own narrative allowed me to be acutely self reflexive regarding my experience. I witnessed how the performer interpreted and eventually embodied my own personal experience. The performance reflected a journey of discovery that I had indeed engaged. The performer's rendition of that process validated the authenticity of my claim of past victimization. My story "fit," it made sense in the overall continuity of the production. In this sense, I experienced a sense of empowerment. Yet, perhaps even more significant, I also experienced a sense or feeling of loss of some kind. As I eventually shared information with the assistant director that I was the narrator on stage, as I owned my own experience, I became quite self conscious and uneasy. It was often difficult to view a rehearsal of the material. I felt very exposed. These feelings prompted me to rethink my initial impressions of the interview sessions with other survivors. How did they feel after disclosing and owning their experiences during the interviews? Did they feel that same sense of loss? Can a survivor feel empowered after claiming survivor status and simultaneously overpower feelings of loss? For me, the loss was lack of confidentiality, personal exposure. My perceptions of myself and my experiences were no longer in my control, they were now performance text. My narrative had a life separate from my own. Staging abuse survivor narratives generated by this research enabled me to confront the fundamental assumptions of the study on a very personal level.

DISCUSSION

The production of "Breaking the Cycle" left me with more questions than answers. There are ethical questions as well as pragmatic questions. For example, did the production actually serve the narrators represented on stage? Was the audience left with a greater understanding of the experiences of the abused?

The re-performance of abuse survivor narratives can serve as an empowering act to the original tellers who explore their own "unfolding story" through narration, as well as the audience members who can empathize with the "collective story" (Richardson, 1990, p. 128) represented on stage. Such a reaction seemed evidenced, somewhat, as members of the audience disclosed how their own experiences mirrored those represented in "Breaking the Cycle," after Audiencing the performances. Richardson (1990) suggests:

> At the individual level, people make sense of their lives through the stories that are available to them, and they attempt to fit their stories into the available stories . . . collective stories which deviate from standard cultural plots provide new narratives, hearing them legitimates a replotting of one's own life. New narratives offer the patterns for new lives. The story of a transformed life, then, becomes a part of the cultural heritage affecting future stories and future lives (p. 129)

"Breaking the Cycle" became a study in possibilities, the possibility of narrator transformation, of narrative empowerment, of greater understanding through the performative act. Significant questions remain. Could this performance have touched the life of just one victim who was encouraged by the stories of survival? Was the performance responsible in its representation of abuse survivors? Who was represented in this production? "Breaking the Cycle" offered victims and survivors of abuse a "collective story" of transformation and empowerment. If we indeed attempt to fit our lives into "available stories," than "Breaking the Cycle" represents a production from which those trapped in a cycle of violence can gain strength, as they construct their own "future stories" of survival.

Chapter Six

Conclusions

Abuse survivors use the narrative act to facilitate change in their lives. By telling their life stories to others, they are able to reconceptualize their experiences and assume empowered performance stances in their lives. Such empowerment is necessary as victims transcend to survivorship. Through narrative performance, abuse survivors can create positive "future stories" (Polkinghorne, 1988) and "alter the direction" of their lives (Richardson, 1990). An analysis of the narratives collected for this study showed that "effective" performances of abuse survivor narratives result in assistance from a support network including family, friends, and service providers. Additionally, and perhaps more importantly, narrative performance was found to be directly related to teller empowerment.

In this study, I examined three questions: What role does narrative risk play in the narratives of abuse survivors? How does the telling of abuse survivor narratives impact the participants in this study? What can we learn about highly disclosive narration through re-performance of abuse survivor narratives? In order to begin answering these questions, I interviewed two populations of survivors including clients of Haven House and self-selected volunteers. The process of data collection, transcription, coding, and analysis yielded answers to the research questions posed by this study. In the following pages, I will assess the role narrative risk plays in the telling of survivor narratives, how the telling of such narratives impacts the tellers, and what was learned through the re-performance of abuse survivor narratives.

NARRATIVE RISK AND THE TELLING OF
ABUSE SURVIVOR NARRATIVES

Narrating abuse survivor narratives can involve personal risk to the teller including psychological stress or the possibility of physical endangerment. To discern fully the roles that narrative risk plays in the narratives of abuse survivors, it is necessary to examine the ways in which the survivors used the narrative event to assist in their move to empowerment. It is through risk taking that narrative empowerment can occur.

During the construction of their narratives, drawn from the interview sessions, I found that the narrators used two categories of themes in their survivor rhetoric. These include themes of disempowerment which can perpetuate silence, and themes of empowerment which can facilitate change.

Nine themes of disempowerment were identified in an analysis of twelve narratives. (1) Traditional roles, which involve an individual's complacency with traditional-patriarchal definitions of acceptable gender performance. Traditional roles often involve dominance and submission manifested in roles of parent, spouse, or child. (2) Relational loyalty, which involves a belief that an individual is obligated to remain silent, ignore, or fail to act regarding the abuse to protect his or her spouse, significant other, parent, sibling, friend, and so forth, merely for the purpose of preserving the relationship they share. (3) Social construction of an abuse victim. This category involves social construction as perceived by the abused, abuser, or other members of a given society. It occurs when an individual does not "fit" into socially accepted ideals of victimization. Consequently, the individual may not be afforded assistance as a victim of abuse. (4) Perceived power dynamics, includes institutional or personal levels of perceived power that can limit the victim's ability to engage in assertive behavior, leave abusive relationships, or narrate their experiences. The power dynamics may involve issues of race, class, gender performance, and so forth. The individual often has low self esteem, is isolated from others, and is demeaned by the abuser. (5) Economic insecurity, which exists when a victim of abuse remains in an abusive relationship because of financial dependence on the abuser. (6) Threat of injury or loss, includes a belief that acting on one's own behalf, engaging in highly personal disclosure, or trying to leave an abusive relationship could result in injury, death, loss of children, loss of status, home, and so forth. (7) Lack of recourse, involves a belief that an abused individual has no recourse (based on a variety of constraints), and, consequently, remains complacent or silent regarding the abuse. The individuals feel hopeless, that they cannot make it on their own. (8) Attachment to the abuser. In this category, the individual is drawn to the abuser because of love, the abuser's need for nurturing, the abuser's personality, or a belief that the abuser will change. This attachment can also include infatuation, obsession, excitement of the relationship, or co-dependency on drugs or alcohol. Finally, (9) Self destruction, occurs when an abuse victim's feeling of hate, anger, or hopelessness lead to negative personal behavior by the victim, which can result in physical or emotional injury to the victim, i.e., abuse of alcohol, drugs, eating disorders.

Themes of disempowerment often involve a positioning of the performative stance that a narrator assumes. For example, when the narrators assume traditional roles or conform to perceived power dynamics imposed on them by their abusers, their performance stance has been reduced to a secondary position. Attitudes of disempowerment, such as feelings of lack of recourse or attachment to the abuser can cast or position victims of abuse in powerless roles of complacency with the abuse. They may believe that they are unable to assume an assertive performance stance for fear that they will lose relationships, status, or perhaps even life itself.

Emergence from disempowering performance stances requires the victim to engage in potentially risky behavior. Disempowering stances, reflected in the rhetoric and/or perceptions of abuse survivors, may convince a victim of abuse that talk is futile or dangerous, and could make the victim remain silent regarding their abuse. Assuming an empowered performance stance involves risk-taking by victims of abuse, as they begin to move to the status of survivor. The abuse survivors interviewed in this study engaged in varying degrees of risk-taking, as they articulated their experience to the staff of Haven House, other members of support networks, and as they retold their personal life stories to me.

Themes of empowerment which can facilitate change, require the narrator to risk exposure, rejection, and the consequences of confronting their own thoughts and feelings regarding their abuse. Themes of empowerment include the following groups. (1) Responsibility to dependents, occurs when the victim beings to view his or her obligation to children/dependents as more significant than the costs of leaving the relationship (not inconsistent with traditional roles). (2) Reconceptualization of the experience, involves a shifting of the blame away from the victim. The victims begin to view themselves as having more self worth. The victims recognize that the abusers are victimizing them and that the victimization cannot be controlled by altering the victim's behavior. (3) Support of a social network, includes availability of financial or personal (i.e., emotional) support of family, friends, institutions, who may provide a place to go, legal representation or other help. (4) Assessing the costs of the relationship, which occurs when the individual recognizes the potential risks of remaining in the relationship, i.e., personal injury or death, and determines that the risks of staying in the relationship are just as significant or more significant than leaving the relationship. (5) Personal achievement, includes a belief that the future holds hope. This is implied in projections of positive plans for the future, i.e., getting a job, going to school, increase in self confidence, and so forth. (6) Confronting uncertainty, involves a struggle between hope and doubt. Even though the survivors have taken steps to secure independent futures, they experience feelings of uncertainty regarding their ability to make it. Overcoming uncertainty can include confronting societal constraints which produce uncertainty, i.e., the individual's perceived importance within a given society. This category is similar to lack of recourse, but usually results in positive actions toward independence from the abuser. (7) Emphasizing alternative roles occurs when the survivors try to highlight alternative roles in their own repertoire of behavior which are distinct from the roles of victimization they share with their abuser. This often involves a reconceptualization of self, i.e., emphasizing the role of mother, a strong individual, and so forth. (8) Rejecting constraints is similar to confronting uncertainty. In this category, the individual rejects constraints which are perceived to be imposed upon members of a given society. This can include financial or legal limitations, or value-laden constructs which can limit a victim's transcendence to survivorship.

Themes of empowerment involve a positioning of the narrator which is indicative of an empowered performance stance, gained by taking narrative risk, the telling of a survivor narrative. While themes of disempowerment can make an individual remain silent regarding their abuse, themes of empowerment can involve a performance stance which brings change to a survivor's life.

Reconceptualizing their experiences or assessing the costs of a relationship can allow survivors to imagine alternative performance possibilities, and consequently encourage survivors to take the risks necessary to gain independence from their abuser. Narrative risk represents an essential step in transcendence, in that, the survivors must name their experiences to themselves or others to bring about change, to embrace empowered performance stances.

The themes of empowerment I found embedded in these narratives suggest that survivors gradually move to greater degrees of empowered performances. For example, support of a social network or reconceptualization of experience can serve as catalysts for initial moves toward empowerment. However, the survivor must then engage in behaviors which involve greater risk, such as confronting uncertainty, assessing the costs of the relationship, or exploring alternative roles. It is through such performative choices (i.e., performing alternative roles, or narrating their experience), that a survivor facilitates even greater empowerment, the ability to remain independent from the abuser.

The language the narrators used in constructing their life stories reflects a struggle between disempowerment and empowerment of the teller. How the tellers position themselves, that is, how they construct their performance stance in their storytelling, can influence both their own and their listeners' understanding of their moves to survivorship. The use of empowering themes and narrative risk-taking seems directly related to the ways in which such narrative construction allows the narrators to reinforce empowering performances in their everyday lives. In the next section, I will discuss how the narrative event impacts the tellers, by invoking narrative sensemaking and performative strategies by the tellers.

THE IMPACT OF THE TELLING

Research on personal narratives suggests that the performance of personal narratives can give meaning to the teller's experience and enhance the teller's self concept. Results of this study indicate that survivors of abuse use the performative act of storytelling to perpetuate change in their lives. Through their storytelling, they can gain self esteem and gain assistance from a social network of friends, family, or service providers. Through a re-performance of their narratives, they can educate others, and continually empower themselves, by reaffirming their decisions to leave their abusive partners and emerge as independent individuals who determine their own life stories.

Telling abuse survivor narratives impacts the teller in two primary ways. First, telling assists the survivors in narrative sensemaking. Secondly, the narratives reinforce empowered stances through the performance strategies the tellers invoke in the act of telling their life stories.

Narrative Sensemaking

Narrative sensemaking refers to the narrators' attempts to understand their experiences more fully by engaging in the act of telling. As they constructed their personal stories, the narrators for this study were able to make sense of their past recollections and current states of awareness regarding their abuse. Through the use of survivor discourse, thematic combinations, and emphasis on dramatic references, the narrators made sense of their experiences.

Survivor discourse is discourse invoked by the tellers which accentuates their perspectives of their experiences. It includes the selection and/or omission of details regarding the abuse, the abusers, or themselves. By selecting specific survivor discourse in their narrative recounting, the narrators aided narrative sensemaking for their listeners as well as themselves, by scrutinizing and justifying the decisions they made and actions they took to bring about change in their lives. This is an important way in which the narrators constructed current perspectives of themselves, for example, to reinforce their empowered statuses, which assisted them in remaining independent of their abusers control.

The narrators for this study used combinations of themes in their survivor narratives. These combinations included the use of two or more recurrent themes of disempowerment, empowerment, or combinations of disempowerment and empowerment themes used concurrently. Thematic combinations, like the use of survivor discourse, involves the positioning of the narrator in the story. For example, tellers' references to past states of disempowerment often yielded to discussions of the empowered statuses to which they eventually emerged. Thematic combinations facilitated sensemaking and guided discussions regarding transcendence by demonstrating how the narrators move from victimization to survivorship. The narrators explored their negative experiences, and through their storytelling, were able to reflect and comment upon how they emerged from disempowerment.

Another method of narrative sensemaking is the narrators' use of dramatic references in their storytelling. By dramatic references, I am referring to the use of emotionally graphic, sensational and/or shocking language and descriptions of narrated events. Using dramatic references reinforces the narrators' decisions to leave their relationships, by focusing on the significant, dangerous incidents they endured. By emphasizing the dramatic, they emphasized the degree to which they were victimized in their relationships. Further, they emphasized the significance of their transcendence to survivorship by demonstrating the serious life dramas that they confronted and eventually overcame.

Finally, narrative sensemaking was aided by the narrators meta-critical recountings of their experiences. These recountings referenced the narrators' past and current perceptions of their states of mind and of their life conditions as they continually move from roles of victims to survivors. Their recountings became a means for the narrators to conceptualize their experiences, as well as accentuate the triumph over adversity in their lives. For example, the narrators' meta-critique allowed them to confront issues in their past which had restricted transcendence. They confronted issues of failing to act sooner to remove themselves from the abusive situations, engaging in negative coping strategies, and a tendency to attribute blame to themselves.

The narrative event impacts the survivors by assisting them in understanding their past experiences of abuse. Their recountings often focused on their involvement in such relationships and a need to understand their lack of control over their abusers' behaviors. Through the telling of their personal stories, the survivors gained a greater sense of "relief" from their past belief of culpability for the abuse. They were able to "forgive" themselves by shifting blame to their abusers. These are important steps which assist in an individual's transcendence from victimization to survivorship. Through the self-critique invoked by the narrative event, the survivors were able to make sense of where they're been and how they have moved to their current, more powerful roles.

Performance Strategies

When telling survivor narratives, storytellers invoke and capitalize on specific performance strategies in an effort to gain a desired response from themselves and their listeners. The resulting perceptions of the narrative event have a positive impact on the teller's self confidence, self esteem, and can validate his or her empowered status. Among the strategies used, which mirror the strategies of theatrically-framed performances, are efforts to create characterization, a convincing story line, and setting the stage for transcendence.

In the narratives collected for this study, I found clearly marked positions or character types for the survivors, their abusers, and their audience. First, the narrators positioned themselves in their storytelling, as the protagonists of their stories. By positioning themselves as the central characters, the narrators assumed empowered roles as survivors. In their talk, the narrators positioned themselves as protagonists by describing themselves as survivors, focusing on positive personal achievements, as well as positive future plans. Additionally, some narrators described the assertive roles they now assume in caring for themselves and their children.

The narrators positioned the abusers as the antagonists. A significant amount of narrative time was taken to recount details about the abusers' behaviors, that clearly positioned them as the antagonists of the stories. While this is not surprising, it is still a significant strategy for empowering the teller. By carefully positioning the abuser as their antagonists, the tellers became convincingly more so the protagonists who facilitated change in their lives, further reducing victim blame.

In addition to positioning the characters in the story being told, the narrators positioned the audience in the performance of their narratives. Such a positioning established a collaborative relationship between the teller and listener who participated in the narrative act. By giving voice to the expectations of their audience, this positioning assisted the narrator in claiming ownership of the story. For example, one narrator suggested that her narrative is for her to tell, her "life history, and it's my place to disclose it." The audience members were positioned as agents of empathy. The narrators in this study enhanced audience empathy by strategically emphasizing survivor discourse which described the severity of their abuse, the limited control they had over their lives, as well as the power the abusers assumed in their relationships.

Positioning the narrator, abuser, and the audience, were important strategies of characterization that ultimately placed the tellers in empowered statuses, not only in the story, but in the storytelling performance as well. The narrators choose how to frame the abusive incidents. When the narrators do so in a way that describes them as strong survivors, they embody that characterization in the performance of their narrative, as well as the performance of everyday life experiences.

Throughout the telling of their narratives, the survivors used convincing story lines regarding victimization and survivorship, constructed in believable and compelling ways, by highlighting the incidents of abuse and outside constraints they overcame in order to emerge to their current states of survival. Performative believability is an important objective in narrative recounting. A desire to be believed is especially significant for a victim of abuse in order to transcend to being a survivor of abuse. If victims cannot convince themselves or others that they are abuse victims, that they are not at fault for their abuse, or that the abuse truly exists, they cannot recast themselves as survivors. Offering compelling details assisted the narrators in constructing convincing story lines. The narrators for this study often selected compelling mini-dramas surrounding their abuse when constructing their story lines, and emphasized their strengths in overcoming the abuse.

Another performative strategy invoked by the narrators was the use of survivor discourse in setting the stage for transcendence. The narrators reflected upon differing stages of transcendence, and perpetuated further transcendence through narrative performance. Stages of transcendence reflected through narrative discourse include initial expository statements regarding the perceived need to transcend, discussions of struggling for transcendence, and the realization that change occurred in their lives. Using the narrative event became an important way in which the narrators set the stage for recollections of transcendence, as well as setting goals for their future.

Through narrative sensemaking and effective storytelling performances, the narrators were able to gain access to a shelter, elicit support from family and friends, and achieve personal empowerment.

RE-PERFORMANCE OF SURVIVOR NARRATIVES

In an effort to understand the telling of highly disclosive narratives more completely through re-performance, we staged a production entitled, "Breaking the Cycle" in the Marion Kleinau Theatre of Southern Illinois University at Carbondale. In this one-act show, excerpts of abuse survivor narratives, poetry, and feminist theory were juxtaposed to create a one hour performance.

Through the process of staging the show, we found that performance and re-performance of narratives rely on similar performative strategies and performance features. When one views the stage as an alternative discourse field, the objectives of performance and re-performance seem very closely aligned. The informants and performers used similar performance texts, invoked similar performance strategies, and sought empathic responses from their audiences.

In post-production critique sessions which occurred at Southern Illinois University, Carbondale, and Purdue University, Calumet, performers reported experiencing unique connections with the informants represented in the text. Audience members emphasized a need to be located on stage, which reinforced our initial belief that inclusivity would be an important way to achieve audience empathy. Audience responses indicated that individual members searched for identifiable images on stage which were consistent with their own images of what victimization and survivorship look like or sound like. Audience responses indicated their need to "fit" the survivors represented on stage into socially-constructed ideals consistent with their own predetermined categories.

Perhaps the greatest lesson learned from staging "Breaking the Cycle" came from the inclusion of my own life story in the performance text. As a result of that decision, I began to confront the fundamental assumptions of my research on a very personal level.

Staging the narratives of abuse survivors allowed us to slow down the process of empowerment, scrutinize it, and understand it more completely. The rehearsal process accentuated the categories of disempowerment and empowerment, which are embedded in the narratives collected for this study, as well as the performance text.

DISCUSSION

Results of this study indicate that narrating experiences of victimization and abuse is not only beneficial, but a necessary step in moving from victim to survivor. The narrators for this study used the narrative event as one mode of transcendence to self empowerment. The narratives collected for this study were re-performances of narratives the survivors performed originally to gain access to a shelter, to receive assistance from family and friends, or to conceptualize their experiences in a way which assisted them in pursuing

independence from their abusers. Each re-telling, became an essential means
for the narrators to become further empowered as survivors of abuse.

The critical role of personal narration in achieving empowerment leaves
those trapped in silence with little recourse, with little assistance to emerge
from abusive relationships. If victims of abuse are unable to share their stories of abuse, if they are unable to name their experiences of victimization to
themselves or others, they will be unable to move to empowered positions.
While narration is by no means the only way in which victims of abuse move
to survivorship, they cannot fully rid themselves of the abusive incidents
without recognizing their past roles of victimization. By acknowledging their
victimization through personal narration, victims are able to recast themselves into powerful independent roles.

Any narrative performance relies to a great extent upon the narrators' performance skills, as they construct convincing story lines, enhanced by believable performances. The notion of required performance skills indicates
that those who posses effective storytelling skills, who conform to their audiences' predetermined images of victimization and abuse, gain the assistance
which is necessary to bring positive change to their lives.

The importance of the teller-listener interaction is significant to abuse survivors. As survivors recount their experiences to others, they become further
empowered, by validating their past experiences, and their current states of
independence from their abusers' control. They are able to use the narrative
event to construct positive plans for their future, that will enable them to remain free from the hold of their abusers. While a positive response by their
listeners was important to the participants in this study, some reported experiencing negative or unsympathetic responses by individuals they approached
for assistance regarding their abuse, in prior performances of their narratives.
Despite the negative responses, these narrators continued to tell their stories.
This seems to indicate that despite the listener's response, the narrative event
is empowering in and of itself. The narrators became empowered by engaging in the narration, and audiencing their own storytelling performances.

IMPLICATIONS FOR FUTURE RESEARCH

While this study served to increase an understanding of risk taking, teller empowerment, and the significance of re-performance in understanding abuse
survivor narratives, more research is needed to assess the pragmatic value of
the performance and re-performance of highly disclosive experiences. For example, when abuse survivors narrate their experiences of victimization, what
are the consequences of unsympathetic listener responses? Must a survivor

construct a narrative so that it remains consistent with the listener's image of abuse, to be afforded the label of survivor? Are stage productions, which seek to "give voice to marginalized groups" (Langellier, 1986) truly assisting the informants whose life stories become performance text? How do productions which focus on intimate disclosure affect their audiences? Do such performances evoke audience empathy or audience complicity with controversial, highly disclosive personal issues? How do victims and survivors audience their narratives once they become performance text? Answers to these questions are not easy to discern. However, confronting these questions is critical as everyday life performances become performance text.

Bibliography

Alcoff, L. & Gray, L. "Survivor discourse: Transgression or recuperation?" *Signs*, 18, (1993) 260–290.

Alexander, P.C., Moore, S., Alexander, E.R. "What is transmitted in the intergenerational transmission of violence?" *Journal of Marriage and the Family*, 53, (1991). 657–668.

Aptheker, B. *Tapestries of life: Women's work, women's consciousness, and the meaning of daily experience*. (Amherst: The University of Massachusetts Press, 1989).

Aristotle, *"The poetics"*. In *Aristotle: The poetics, "Longinus": On the sublime, Demetrius: On Style*, ed. T.E. Page, E. Capps, W.H.D. Rouse.W. Hamilton Fyfe (trans.) (New York: G.P. Putnam's Sons, 1932).

Bahm, C. Broda. In L.L. Montalbano and C. Broda-Bahm "Bruising and healing all over again: Staging survivor narratives" (paper presented to the Speech Communication Association. New Orleans, LA: November, 1994).

Bakhtin, M.M. "Discourse in the novel". In *The dialogic imagination*, ed. In M. Holoquist (Ed.), C. Emerson & M. Holoquist (Trans.). (Austin: University of Texas Press, 1981). 260–275.

Barnes, J.A. "Who should know what?" *Social Science Privacy and Ethics*. Harmondsworth: Penguin. In *Doing research on sensitive topics.*, ed. R. Lee (Newbury Park, CA: Sage, 1993) 260–275.

Barthes, R. "Introduction to the structural analysis of narratives". In *Image-music-text*, ed. S. Heath (New York: Hill and Wang, 1977) 79–124.

Bauman, R. "American folklore studies and social transformation: A performance-centered perspective". *Text and Performance Quarterly*, 9, (1989) 175–184.

——. The field study of context. In *Handbook of American folklore*, ed. R.M. Dorson (Bloomington: Indiana University Press, 1983) 362–368.

——. *Story, performance, event: Contextualized studies of oral narrative*. (Cambridge: Cambridge University Press, 1986).

Bennet, G. (1986). "Narrative as expository discourse" *Journal of American Folklore*, 99 (1986), 415–434.

Bochner, A.P. "Narrative Virtues". *Qualitative Inquiry*, 7, (2001) 131–157.

Browne, A. In *Behind closed doors: Family violence in the home. July 9, 1991.U.S. Senate Subcommittee on children, family, drugs and alcoholism of the Committee on Labor and Human Resources*. (Washington, D.C.: U.S. Government Printing Office, 1991) (No. iii, 93 p. :ill. 24cm).

Capo, K.E. & Hantzis, D. "(En) Gendered (and endangered) subjects: Writing, reading, performing, and theorizing feminist criticism." *Text and Performance Quarterly*, 9, (1991) 243–276.

Chatman, S. *Story and discourse: Narrative structure in fiction and film*. (New York: Ithaca, 1978).

Collins, P. Hill. *Black feminist thought: Knowledge, consciousness, and the politics of empowerment. Perspectives on gender, volume 2*. (New York: Routeledge, 1991).

Conquergood, D. (1985). "Performing as a moral act: Ethical dimensions of the ethnography of performance." *Literature in Performance*, (1985) 5, 1–13.

———. "Rethinking ethnography: Towards a critical cultural politics." *Communication Monographs*, 58, (1991) 179–194.

———. "A sense of the other: Interpretation and ethnographic research". In *Proceedings of the seminar conference on oral traditions*, eds. I. Crouch & G. Owen. (New Mexico: New Mexico State University, 1983) 148–155.

Danica, E. *Don't: A woman's word*. (San Francisco, CA: Cleis Press, 1988).

Denzin, N.K. "Toward a phenomenology of domestic family violence." *American Journal of Sociology*, 90, (1984) 483–513.

Denzin, D.K & Lincoln, Y.S. *Handbook of qualitative research*. 2nd. Ed. (Thousand Oaks, CA: Sage, 2000).

Dodd, C.J. (1991). "*Behind closed doors: Family violence in the home. July 9, 1991. U.S. Senate Subcommittee on children, family, drugs, and alcoholism of the Committee on Labor and Human Resources*" (Washington, D.C.: U.S. Government Printing Office, 1991). (No. iii, 93 p. ill.: 24cm.).

Duranti, A. & Brenneis, D. (Eds.), "The audience as co-author. " Special edition of *Text*, 6, (1986) 239–247.

Dworkin, A. *Intercourse*. (New York: The Free Press, 1987).

Fine, E.C. *The folklore text: From performance to print*. (Bloomington: Indiana University Press, 1984).

Fine, E.C. & Speer, J.H. "A new look at performance."*Communication Monographs*, 44, (1977) 374–389.

Fisher, W. *Human communication as narration: Toward a philosophy of reason, value, and action*. (Columbia: University of South Carolina Press, 1989).

———. "Narration as a human communication paradigm: The case of public moral argument." *Communication Monographs*, 51, (1984) 1–22.

Frank, A. W. "The standpoint of the storyteller." *Qualitative Health Research*, 10, (2000) 354–365.

———. *The wounded storyteller: Body, illness, and ethics*. (Chicago: The University of Chicago Press, 1995).

Geffner, R., Rosebaum, A., & Hughes, H. "Research issues concerning family violence." In *Handbook of family violence*, eds. V.B. Van Hasselt, R.L. Morrison, A.S. Bellach, M. Hersen (New York: Plenum Press, 1988) 319–358.

Goffman, E. *The presentation of self in everyday life*. (Garden City: Doubleday, 1959).

Hoff, L. A. *Battered women as survivors*. (New York: Routeledge, 1990).

Hutchings, N. *The violent family: Victimization of women, children, and the elderly*. (New York: Human Science Press, 1988).

Holoquist, M. "The glossary." In The dialogic imagination, eds. M. Holoquist, C. Emerson & M. Holoquist (Trans.), (Austin: The University of Texas Press, 1981) 423–434.

Kerby, A. P. *Narrative and the self*. (Bloomington: Indiana University Press, 1991).

Kirkwood, W. G. "Narrative and the rhetoric of possibility." *Communication Monographs*, 59, (1992) 30–47.

Langellier, K. "A phenomenological approach to the audience." *Literature in Performance*, 3, (1983) 34–39.

———. "From text to social context." *Literature in Performance*, 6, (1986) 60–70.

———. "Personal narratives in performance." In *Renewal and Revision: The future of interpretation*, ed. T. Colson (Denton, TX: NB Omega, 1986) 132–144.

———. "Personal narrative, performance, performativity: Two or three things I know for sure." *Text and Performance Quarterly*, 17, (1999) 125–144.

———. "Personal narratives: Perspectives on theory and research. *Text and Performance Quarterly*, 9, (1989) 243–276.

Langellier, K & Hall, D. "A phenomenological approach to feminist communication research." In, *Doing research in women's communication: Perspectives on theory and research*, eds. C. Spitzack & K. Carter (Norwood, NJ: Ablex, 1989) 193–220.

Lawson, J.H. *Theory and technique of playwriting*. (New York: Hill and Wang, 1960).

Lee, R. *Doing research on sensitive topics*. (Newbury Park, CA: Sage, 1993).

Loseke, D. R. *The battered and shelters: The social construction of wife abuse* (Albany: State University of New York Press, 1992).

Lucaites, J.L. & Condit, C.M. "Re-constructing narrative theory: A functional perspective". *Journal of Communication*, 35, (1983) 90–108.

Mandelbaum, J. "Interpersonal activities in communication storytelling." *Western Journal of Speech Communication*, 53, (1989) 114–126.

Nelson, J.L. "Phenomenology as feminist methodology: Explicating interviews." In *Doing research in women's communication: Perspectives on theory and research*, eds. C. Spitzack & K. Carter, (Norwood, NJ: Ablex, 1989) 221–241.

NiCarthy, G. *The ones who got away: Women who left their abusive partners*. (Seattle: The Seal Press, 1987).

Norton, C. Sullivan. *Life metaphors: Stories of ordinary survival*. (Carbondale, IL: Southern Illinois University Press, 1989).

Ong, W.J. "Oral remembering and narrative structures." In *Analyzing discourse: Text and talk, ed.* Deborah Tannen. (Washington, D.C.: Georgetown University Press, 1982) 12–24.

Park-Fuller, L. "Narrative and narratization of a cancer story: Composing and performing, *A Clean Breast of It*." *Text and Performance Quarterly*, 15, (1995) 60–67.

Pelias, R.J. *Performance studies: Interpretation of aesthetic texts*. (New York: St. Martin's Press, 1992).

Peled, I., Jaffe, P.G. & Eddleson, J.L. (Eds.). *Ending the cycle of violence: Community responses to children of battered women*. (Thousand Oaks, CA: Sage, 1995).

Peterson, E.E. & Langellier, K. "The politics of personal narrative methodology." *Text and Performance Quarterly,* 17, (1997) 135–152.

Peterson, E.E. & Langellier, K. "The risk of performing personal narratives." In *On narratives: Proceedings of the 10th international colloquium on speech communication,* ed. H. Geissner (Frankfurt Germany: Scriptor, 1986) 98–115.

Piercy, M. "Rape poem". In *Poetspeak: In their work, about their work,* ed. P.B. Janeczko, (New York, NY: Collier Books, 1991).

Polkinghorne, D. *Narrative knowing and the human sciences.* (Albany: State University of New York Press, 1988).

Presnell, M. "Narrative gender differences: Orality and literacy."In *Doing research on women's communication: Perspectives on theory and research,* eds. C. Spitzack and K. Carter (Norwood, NJ: Ablex, 1989) 221–241.

Plummer, K. *Telling sexual stories: Power, change, and social worlds.* New York: Routeledge, 1995.

Richardson, L. "Narrative and Sociology." *Journal of Contemporary Ethnography,* 19, (1990) 116–135.

Riessman, C.K. *Narrative Analysis.* (Newbury park, CA: Sage, 1993).

Robinson, J.A. "Personal narratives reconsidered." *Journal of American Folklore,* 94, (1981) 58–95.

Sartre, J.P. "What is literature?" In *Playwriting: The structure of action,* ed. S. Smiley. B. Frechtman (Trans.) (Englewood Cliffs, New Jersey: Prentice-Hall, Inc, 1971), 3.

Schechner, R. "Toward a poetics of performance." *Essays on Performance theory.* (New York: Drama Books Specialists, 1977).

Scholes, R. "Language, narrative, and anti-narrative." In *On narrative,* ed. W.J.T. Mitchell (Chicago: University of Chicago Press, 1981).

Sedlak, J. "Prevention of wife abuse." In *Handbook of family violence,* eds. V.B. Van Hasselt, R.L. Morrison, A.S. Bellach, M. Hersen. (New York: Plenum Press, 1988) 319–358.

Smiley, S. *Playwriting: the structure of action.* (Englewood Cliffs, NJ: Prentice-Hall, Inc, 1971).

Smith, B. Herrnstein. " Narrative versions, narrative theories." In *On narrative,* ed. W.J.T. Mitchell (Chicago: University of Chicago Press, 1981) 209–232.

Spitzack, C. & Carter, K. "Research on women's communication: The politics of theory and method." In *Doing research in women's communication: Perspectives on theory and research,* eds. C. Spitzack & K. Carter. (Norwood, NJ: Ablex, 1989) 11–39.

Stahl, S.K.D. "Personal experience stories." In *Handbook of American Folklore,* ed. M. Dorson, (Bloomington: Indiana University Press, 1983) 268–276.

Strauss, A. & Corbin, J. *Basics of qualitative research.* (Newbury Park, CA: Sage, 1990).

Stucky, N. "Toward an aesthetics of natural performance." *Text and Performance Quarterly,* 13, (1993)168–180.

Sullivan. C. "Transcending everyday life through narrative communication: Stories that help us cope." In *On narratives: Proceedings of the 10th international colloquium on speech communication*, ed. H. Geissner (Frankfurt, Germany: Scriptor, 1986) 116–129.

Swenson, M. "Bleeding." In *The Norton anthology of literature by women: The tradition in English*, eds. S.M. Gilbert and S. Gubar (New York, NY: W.W. Norton and Company, 1985).

Turner, V. "Address to planning committee for upcoming conferences." In *By means of performance; Intercultural studies on theatre and ritual*, eds. R. Schechner and W. Appel. (Cambridge: Cambridge University Press, 1991).

——, *From ritual to theatre: The human seriousness of play*. (New York: PAJ Publications, 1982).

——, "Social dramas and stories about them." In *On narrative, ed.* W.J.T. Mitchell. (Chicago: University of Chicago Press 1981) 137–164.

Uniform Crime Reports, Federal Bureau of Investigation *Myths and facts on domestic violence*. Retrieved: October 26, 2000: (http://www.famvi.com/dv facts.htm,1991).

United States Commission on Civil Rights. *Battered women: Iissues of public policy*. (Washington, D.C.: U. S. Government Printing Office, 1978).

Walker, A. "In search of our mother's gardens." In P. H. Collins *Black feminist thought*. (New York; Routeledge, 1991).

Ward, K. "The importance of the interaction of gender, race, and class in the recasting of sociological theory: Reply toWilson." In *Theory on gender/feminism on theory*, ed. P. England. (New York: Aldine DeGruyler, 1993) 365–366.

Wiggins, J.A. "Family violence as a case of interpersonal aggression: A situational analysis." *Social Forces*, 62, (1983) 102–123.

Zinn, M. Baca, L. Weber Cannon, E. Higginbotham, & B. Thorton Dill."The costs of exclusionary practices in women's studies." *Signs*, 11, (2), (1986) 290–303.

Index